FACING CH
CHA

FACING CHANGES

CHANGING FACES

Positive
Spiritual and Emotional Growth
in Mid-Life

ALVIN MARCETTI AND SHIRLEY LUNN

DARTON·LONGMAN+TODD

First published in 1995 by
Darton, Longman and Todd Ltd
1 Spencer Court
140–142 Wandsworth High Street
London SW18 4JJ

ISBN 0–232–52082–8

A catalogue record for this book is available from the British
Library

Phototypeset in 10/12^1/$_2$pt Palatino by
Intype, London

Printed and bound in Great Britain by
Redwood Books, Trowbridge, Wiltshire

We cannot live the afternoon of life according to the programme of life's morning; for what was great in the morning will be little at evening, and what in the morning was true will at evening have become a lie.

C.G. Jung

Contents

Acknowledgements

Of course this book could not have been written without the shared experiences of the many mid-life men and women with whom we have worked over the years. I would like particularly to thank those who were willing to have their stories used in the text, although the names and situations are often changed. My grateful thanks must be given to Revd Mark Sutherland, Chaplain at the Maudsley Hospital, London, for his comments on the manuscript from a pyschodynamic perspective, and the Revd Andre Feuz, pastor of the Church of Zurich congregation in Enge, who provided some much-needed quiet space for writing in Zurich. My collaborator, Shirley Lunn, has contributed more to this project than she realizes and without her patience and her ability to rein in my often exuberant prose the text would have been much less readable. I must also acknowledge my therapeutic relationship with John Goodchild, which has been instrumental in my own mid-life renegotiation.

ALVIN MARCETTI
Zurich, May 1994

Prologue

In our first book, *A Place of Growth: Care and Counselling of People with AIDS*, we seduced the reader into reading the Introduction by making it the first chapter. Those of you who have read this book will already know a good deal about the authors, as it is as much about our own personal journeys with HIV/AIDS as it is about patient care and counselling. In *Facing Changes: Changing Faces*, we are taking more of a risk that you may skip over this Prologue, but it is a place where we can talk directly to the reader about ourselves and our assumptions in writing this book.

First of all, we want to come out of the closet, lay our cards on the table, or however you might like to put it: both of us are mid-lifers, a middle-aged man and woman who have shared a close personal and professional relationship for the past eight years. We both have partners of long standing, children, complex family ties, and a shared deep Christian faith. In addition to these mutual qualities we also share the belief that the beginning of mid-life is the most creative and exciting time for most men and women if they have the courage to make use of the challenges presented to them. On the dedication page you read the quote by C.G. Jung about reordering the programme of one's life to suit the afternoon rather than the morning. This is a lovely way of looking at the process we call mid-life renegotiation; and one which puts the task in positive perspective.

Mid-life has been a creative time for both of us and much of our personal journeys is shared in the text which follows, as are the experiences of the countless men and women with whom we have worked over the years. Shirley has been a wife, mother, caring daughter and lover in the morning of her life. Her afternoon has been characterized by new challenges in both her marriage and her professional life. She returned to work after raising a family and found herself quite quickly at the centre of building something that had never existed before, a Christian AIDS hospice. Her mid-life changes have opened opportunities to travel, to teach and to lecture around the world and an opportunity to meet people far beyond her previous experience as a suburban housewife and mother. While her traditional Christian faith has remained a foundation for her daily life her spirituality has changed and broadened in mid-life to include an appreciation of sacramental theology and other faith traditions.

Alvin left a successful teaching career in the States in his late thirties to train for ministry and came halfway around the world to study and to work in the Church of England. He has been obedient son, unsuccessful husband, faithful friend, successful lover and caring parent; these experiences have been the foundation for a renewed mid-life which has taken him to holy orders, ministry in the East End of London, ten years of travel around the world and now life as university chaplain at London Guildhall University and author. His Christian faith, embedded in the catholic tradition of Anglicanism, has provided the underpinning of an exciting and continuing afternoon of life.

One of the gifts of mid-life renegotiation is the realization that there are no easy answers to the complex questions and problems of life. This is not a 'quick fix' recipe book for mid-life change. What you will find in the text that follows are the experiences of men and women who have begun to live the afternoon of life courageously and with renewed hope. By letting go of the pain of the past, the failures and successes, we find that men and women are able to move forward creatively by setting new goals. These goals, and the activities which form the living out of them, are most often person-centred rather than achievement-focused. We often hear talk of the 'greying' of the Western democracies which means that those of us born after the War are now largely middle aged. There are a lot of us about, and there is a need to explore the personal implications of ageing and the effect it has on our spirituality and emotional growth. We invite you to listen to the voices of the scores of men and women who have contributed their stories to *Facing Changes: Changing Faces*. Some of the voices tell their stories directly, and many others are anonymous contributors through sharing their journeys with the authors. You will find in this book some common themes, and it is best to state them up front. They include a commitment to traditional Christian belief, an appreciation of the use of psychotherapy and counselling in negotiating mid-life change, the absolute value of balancing one's spirituality with one's emotional life, and the importance of sharing intimacy with other men and women.

One of the most freeing aspects of mid-life is embodied in the poem by Rilke which closes this book (p. 156). He speaks of living life in growing orbits which circle around God for a thousand years and still not knowing if he is falcon, storm, or a great song. Letting go of the need for specific answers to unanswerable questions is one of the necessary and freeing challenges of mid-life, and it is only then that we may begin to realize that we are part of God's great song.

1

FACING CHANGES

'I was so young once; just look!' The woman opened her bag and searched for a small faded photograph and handed it across to her colleague. 'Can you believe that I was once that? I can't even remember what it felt like . . . and now I look in the mirror and I see this!' Her eyes brimmed for a moment as she stared wistfully at the small brown tinted photo booth image from the 1950s.

This poignant story is repeated again and again in consulting rooms, vicar's studies, over coffee with a friend, or a counsellor's office, throughout the developed world. Men and women caught in the tensions of negotiating the challenges of the second phase of life seek out the counsel of someone they can trust. They come to share their *angst*, pain and confusion as well as their shame and guilt at feeling the loss of youthful vigour and the almost self-obsessed energy which most people feel well into their thirties. For some this will herald the time which is often called the 'mid-life crisis', a term which the authors reject from the outset. There is an inherent mistake in seeing change and growth in mid-life as a crisis, and how we are guided during this time always has a direct effect on the quality of the second half of our lives. Perhaps the real danger lies in giving a pseudo-medical label to the period of transition which begins somewhere in the early thirties for most people. The danger of the medical model is that we can come to see ourselves as sick, as patients in the great hospital of middle age. A more positive and creative label for this period, if we must have one, is mid-life renegotiation and the time should be seen as part of the natural process of life.

This process of renegotiation is an ongoing one, and it is

1

dangerous to see ourselves as getting over the hurdle of mid-life crisis. Such an attitude can lead us to believe that life will settle down and that there will be easy sailing from here on. It might be pleasant if that were so, but the experience of most mature men and women is that this is not the case. In our roles as pastoral and clinical counsellors, we have seen hundreds of men and women over the years and our observation is that the onset of mid-life renegotiation is actually the beginning of a continuous process which takes the rest of one's life. This may sound a bit ominous to some, but there is great creativity and challenge in knowing that life is a series of growth periods layered between quieter, more settled times where one can enjoy the fruits of the work which has preceded the calm. The joy comes from knowing that somewhere along the road there will be some new learning and changing to be done. Life is never over, never fixed; and it is a good thing that it is not. For people of faith this should not come as a surprise as Scripture is full of men and women who experience life as process, rather than stasis. The God known by Christians is one who creates life anew within each one of us in a unique manner; what we do with this creative work begun by God is up to us.

The woman grasping the image of her faded youth is not a sad example of someone who has been unable to let go of a glorious past: she is a woman who, due to her unusual beauty in early life, negotiates that loss on a continual basis; while there is sadness contained within the process there is also a sharp edge to the loss which in some way gives meaning to the present. It must be said that Jane, the woman about whom we are speaking, is a very beautiful sixty-year-old. She has a sense of style, wit and charm which has not diminished in any way over the years, and she seems to have the uncanny gift of always choosing the most flattering and dramatic clothes which affirm her personality without exhibiting any lust for lost youth. Her maturity is a counterpoint to her beauty as it is clear to even the casual observer that she has always been a beautiful woman. Jane is one of the courageous ones who see life as a continual negotiation of loss, change and new growth.

Amanda tells a similar story, but she is a woman who has experienced her beauty as a negative gift and has struggled throughout her life to escape the burden which it brought. This physical gift has been a dominant motif in Amanda's life, one which has brought her much pain while being an important component in her several successful careers. Ageing has been a particular problem for Amanda since her beauty was bound to change as she moved into her middle years. In her early life so many things 'came easy' as she has always lived in a society which places complex emphasis on physical appearance. At the same time it was difficult for Amanda to establish herself in academic life because she was bound by the double chains of beauty and high intelligence. For years she fought to be taken seriously by male colleagues and found herself at times attempting to play down her appearance by wearing unflattering clothes and no jewellery or make-up while working. Then she would recreate herself to pursue her personal life as a beautiful, desirable woman. This tension between the two Amandas resulted in a early life typified by depression and insecurity.

Depression is much more common in early life than in mid-life, contrary to the negative myths about middle age, and it was this depression which first brought Amanda to counselling and then to psychotherapy. In fact, counselling has been one of the constants in Amanda's life, and rather than seeing it as dependency she has courageously moved through her life going in and out of therapeutic relationships which have enabled her to live more fully.

The process of moving in and out of counselling/therapy brings up the idea that life can be seen as a series of adjustments to new situations in which we find ourselves due to the ageing process. When we leave school or university the focus of our lives often takes the form of two priorities: establishing ourselves in a lasting, personal relationship and establishing ourselves in a career. There is an intensity about the early years after school which does not occur at any other time in our lives. We become so focused on the twin goals of career and relationship that time is usually not given to planning for the future, accepting that we must age, or taking on board that life will change as we grow older. Many people enter their middle thirties and are surprised by the fact they will die some day, that their hair is thinning and that their bodies are thickening. These are not stupid or insensitive people, but merely people who have put their major energies into the appropriate work of the early years. There is an important distinction to be made between knowing intellectually the facts just mentioned and experiencing them on an emotional level. The fact that the work of the early years is so product-oriented often prevents us from realizing the other dimensions of life: the spiritual and emotional. This is not to say that the early years are not times of intense emotions. This is a time when we may experience the first deep love of our lives, our first important sexual experiences, the joy of new birth when children become part of a relationship and the sense of accomplishment when we are successful in finding work and becoming established. For gay men and women the early years are often consumed with accepting and exploring what it means to be gay in a heterosexual world. The joy of coming to terms with the giveness of one's sexuality is often offset by the pain of realizing that we will always be an outsider in mainstream culture with its emphasis on family life. Exploring the reality of same-sex relationships and the search for appropriate models is the work many gay people find themselves involved with in their twenties.

The onset of mid-life can be fixed anywhere between the ages of thirty and forty-five, and writers in the field all seem to have some favourite age to argue. Some say that men often experience a great need for change at the age of forty-two, and research studies in the United States have pursued this idea. Others feel that the early thirties are a time when people begin to re-examine the goals they have set for themselves and to renegotiate plans for the future. Women often experience a sense of mid-life change if they have had their children young. Family life begins to change in their late thirties when the children begin to leave home. We believe that all these theories are true, but we believe more importantly that mid-life is not a physical moment in one's journey but rather that a more spiritual or emotional time frame is required to view the process clearly. Mid-life is not only about the ageing process – although this can be an important influence – but about beginning to live the examined life. This can occur at almost any time in one's life, but for the reasons stated earlier it is most typically seen when we are established for a time in our careers and personal life. We begin to look at what we have planned for goals and to evaluate whether we have reached them or not. One young New Zealand sheep farmer said he wanted to be a millionaire by the time he was forty and felt greatly disappointed because he was only worth three-quarters of a million by that age. The pain of the failure to achieve the often unrealistic goals of early life form a theme for renegotiations in our middle years. Mid-life can occur quite early or be staved off by circumstance until the early or mid-forties for both men and women. This middle part of our lives can be the most creative and fulfilling time as we have a past of success and failure on which to build an enlivened future. Contrary to accepted belief, mid-life is just this kind of experience for many people when accompanied by spiritual and emotional examination. This process continues until well into the late fifties when we are faced with the new challenge of old age, or the third stage of life as the authors like to envision it. While not the subject of this book, there is much to be written about the third stage of life and many myths which need to be banished, beginning with the view that people beyond sixty are OAPs with little potential for growth and whose particular challenge is monitoring a deteriorating physical body. However, that is a subject for subsequent writing.

One of the first tasks faced by someone entering mid-life is the evaluation of one's interior and exterior lives. When this is done honestly and without a sense of failure or doom, the challenge of mid-life can be taken up. The thirty-five-year-old must look at professional accomplishments to see if they match up with youthful ambition. Our New Zealand farmer mentioned earlier found some pain in knowing that he would not achieve his goal by forty, but he was able to realize how much he had accomplished in fifteen years – 10,000 head of sheep grazing on 5,000 acres of land which he owned outright, a modest but comfortable home, a family life which gave his demanding role on the farm meaning, and a significant amount of cash on deposit. By holding the two in balance, the dream and the reality, he is able to make plans for the future without punishing himself for falling short of a goal set when he was a different person. What this simple example

5

illustrates is the process of what we call learning to be true to the good inside of us. Let us illustrate this fuzzy concept with another concrete example.

Paula describes herself as 'a wild child' when speaking about her adolescence and early life. She has little bad to say about her upbringing and feels that her parents were good, loving people who always wanted the best for her and her brothers and sisters. The other three children thrived in this environment, but Paula felt she never fitted with her ordinary, caring family. At school she was constantly on report and was moved several times. As she entered her teenage years she began running away from home for a variety of reasons.

> I guess I wanted attention, and I found it so boring just being me with my nice, dull family. There was nothing exciting in my life so I went looking for it. What I found was a lot of other young people like myself living on the streets and creating an under-world which existed alongside but not as part of mainstream life. Within a few weeks it wasn't so exciting; it was cold, lonely and I got tired of begging, so I would go home. But sooner or later I'd run away again because the lure of the streets was too exciting. My parents just couldn't cope, and I tried to get them to accept that I wasn't worth all their trouble, that there must be some kind of badness inside me which made me do the things I did.

Paula's parents tried everything from counselling to boarding school, but in the end they just had to give up and let Paula go her own way. She left home for good when she was eighteen and took a job as a waitress in London.

The next few years were like one long American soap opera full of short-term lovers, unwanted pregnancies, a bad marriage, experiments with drugs and drifting from one menial job to another. In an attempt to give some meaning to her life, Paula did an access course with an idea to train as a teacher, but she soon lost interest. This was followed by a relationship with an Australian man who took her travelling around the world where her pattern of broken relationships, uninteresting and poorly paid work, and a sense that just floating from one trauma to the next was the way life was supposed to be.

I don't know what made me think about where I was going with my life. Maybe it was turning thirty, or maybe it was my last relationship which was with a man ten years younger than me. He left me with our son, Jason, saying that he didn't want to be saddled with an old wife when he was thirty. It wasn't the fact that he left that was hurtful or what he said about me being old, but I began to realize that I was no longer a kid, but I saw no way to change. I was convinced that the 'wild child' inside me had control forever. My ever-faithful parents asked me to come home with Jason and give myself time to think things over. I had no choice, so I accepted.

The visit home gave Paula a window of time to examine her life, to discuss her feelings with people who had known her for a lifetime. By this time her parents had moved far beyond any attempts at advice-giving or judgement which was an important aspect of Paula's mid-life renegotiation.

It was like a holiday camp for me and Jason. Of course the grandparents were all over him, and I just luxuriated in clean sheets, regular meals, and time to spend by myself. I thought a few times about going back to counselling but I didn't have the money and it had never worked before. I just slept, ate and talked with my Mom and Dad. All they did was listen and sometimes they cried because I told them a lot about my life. My Mom kept saying that I was so hard on myself, that I wasn't a bad person, and that the important thing was that I be happy with the choices I'd made. That was just the problem; I wasn't happy with the choices I'd made, and I was sure that I wasn't capable of making good choices for me and Jason. I realized that I had always been looking for something or someone to give meaning to my life; I'd even tried religion for a while. I felt that there was so much confusion inside me that I would never be able to figure out what I wanted. The time at home was important because for some reason during walks and time by myself the confusion inside began to settle down; I began to see some good things about myself. I'd sit down and say, 'Paula, what do you want? Paula, what's good about you?', and surprisingly enough I began to hear some answers. One of the key events in that time was when I challenged my mother when she said I wasn't a bad person. I think she must have been fed up with me by this time. She sat down at the kitchen table and listed about five things that were good about me: 'Paula, you have a great spirit of adventure, you're a survivor, people are drawn to you and you are able to be useful to them, and you are a good mother to Jason'. I listened this time and I thought that this was really quite a lot of good things. And I took it from there.

The woman who sat telling this story was a smartly dressed teacher in her early forties. No one would ever think that this Paula had been a rootless wanderer for the first half of her life. With the help of her parents, she finished her access course and trained as a teacher. Because she loved travelling and couldn't think of giving it up, she also improved at and added languages to her course. When she left training college her first job was in an international school in France; from there she and Jason moved to Switzerland where she taught languages in an American high school. In her forties she returned to England to take a post as co-ordinator for international students at one of the London universities. This may seem like a romantic success story; Cinderella finally discovered by the prince charming of mid-life, but it must be understood that Paula is a woman of high intelligence and drive; she had not focused those qualities in the first stage of life, but by allowing herself to accept a healing relationship with her parents she was able to touch the good qualities inside of herself. This concept of the healing relationship is an important one. For Paula it was with her parents, with others it may be a spiritual director, a psychotherapist, a friend, or even a lover. One of the ways that God speaks to us is through the people who enter our lives; how we make use of those people is for us to decide. In mid-life the time is often fortuitous, and a window of opportunity like Paula's is presented to us. The inner voice which we hear, and which affirms our goodness, as we evaluate the first stage of life comes both from the mind and the soul. The healing relationship, like Paula's, is often characterized by non-judgemental love, lack of judgement and expectations and assurance that we are worth the time and attention given.

One of the real challenges of the initial stage of mid-life renegotiation is the need to see ourselves in a positive light. Sometimes this comes quite naturally to well-integrated people who have met with success in their early lives, but for most of us there is some residual deposit of guilt about not being worthy. The focus of this for Christians can often be seen as feeling not 'good enough' for God, and there can be a need for re-examining one's model of God. It is all too easy to concentrate on the sacrifice of Christ and the fallen nature of humankind while forgetting that the essential nature of God revealed in Scripture and the tradition of the Church is that of a loving creator who meets people where they are on their life journey. One of the subtle, but quite real, problems for Christians is that we have no model of mid-life in the New Testament. Jesus died when he was thirty-three, and while his human existence is one of inspiration for us, we are not able to draw on a model of middle age. Participation in organized religion can be seen as an obligation rather than as an expression of thanksgiving for life and those around us, and when feeling negative about our reality we can use religious expression to support a negative view of our potential and accomplishments. In our emotional lives parents play the most significant role in our early years. Whether we are willing to acknowledge it or not, many of the choices we make in our twenties are determined by our family experiences. We can react against our family training and choose an 'unacceptable' partner or career choice, or become over-accommodating and make conscious or unconscious choices which will please our parents.

One of the authors had a boyhood dream of training as a foreign correspondent, travelling the world reporting on exciting events in exotic countries, which would release him from the dull monotony of small-town American life. Outwardly his parents encouraged him but there was an unwritten agenda for conformity, and it is not surprising that, while in the last year of university, he chose to train as a teacher and to make a respectable marriage to a fellow student. There followed fifteen pleasant years teaching adolescents how to write and to dream of becoming foreign correspondents. Inside, the young man who longed for adventure, excitement and creativity was kept on a short emotional

9

leash until finally, as he approached forty, the adult began to touch the boyhood dreams which had been put aside and to feel that they were good. The story does not have a Hollywood ending; there was no job waiting on *The Times* or with Reuters, but the man and the boy inside have travelled the world and they do write books.

How, then, does a major life change like this come about, and does mid-life examination always result in dramatic changes of direction? Much of the popular writing and depictions of mid-life change in film and on television would lead us to believe that this is true; however, the reality is much more varied. Of course, people do make dramatic changes in mid-life. The housewife becomes a counsellor, the university counsellor becomes a carpenter, the successful civil servant becomes a landscape gardener, and the high powered business woman becomes a mother at forty. These scenarios do happen and the people who live them out always speak with affirmation about the changes they have made in their lives; what they say almost universally is that the reality of the change was not what they expected at all, but they are grateful they had the courage to make the change. However, it is much more common to look at one's life, to make small but significant adjustments, and to continue living the future much like the past, but with a renewed sense of purpose and meaning. The housewife whose children are grown begins an access course and eventually does a degree course, couples renegotiate their relationships and find they can build on past history to find new ways of relating, the man who knows there will be no more promotions uses the new freedom to take up outside activities he denied himself before. The impetus for these changes can come either from inside or outside. Many people report a sense of ennui, or emotional uneasiness, rather than depression as they began to achieve the first goals they had set for themselves. When we have found a partner and a meaningful career there is a time of building and consolidating those accomplishments which is often followed by the aforementioned ennui. Questions like, 'Is this it?' or 'Where do I go from here?' are more common than, 'I feel desperately trapped in a life without meaning'. It is at this point that many people seek out friends, a clergyperson or perhaps enter psychotherapy in an attempt to get to know the person inside themselves. The energy which was previously used to achieve goals can be focused towards a discovery of self, and this discovery often leads to change.

Events outside our control can begin a mid-life negotiation as well. The death of a close friend or parent can trigger a search for meaning in life. Many people are filled with regrets and guilt when a parent dies, and this is a common situation which brings people to a counsellor. Redundancy as well as professional success, divorce, major illness, and children leaving home are among the many events which can lead us to a re-examination of our goals. Perhaps the most important part of the process is how we see ourselves: as a victim of circumstance or as someone open to challenge when the circumstances of life change. A sense of one's own personal power is an important asset when faced with the beginning of mid-life renegotiation. The opportunity of the discovery or affirmation of the good which lies within us is the gift we are all given. The challenge of this sense of our personal goodness is to face change courageously.

Facing change with courage is not always an easy task, and it is common to become overwhelmed by the work ahead. Not everyone greets it with joy, especially since we are loaded down with negative ideas about the period we are calling mid-life. It is easy to believe that the middle years are characterized by depression, divorce, affairs outside permanent relationships, and that the entire period is marked by a deep sense of dissatisfaction. But new research studies both here and in the United States have contributed some very startling information which seems to negate most of the commonly held myths about middle age. The image of the middle-aged man who attempts to validate his flagging sense of virility with a string of extra-marital affairs with significantly younger women while his wife suffers year after year of menopausal depression is perhaps the most common idea of mid-life. However, the facts seem to contradict this view. In fact, most depression occurs between the ages of twenty-five and thirty-five for single men and women, and one study found that married women show less evidence of depression as each decade goes by. Similar statistics contradict popular views on infidelity and divorce. Most divorces do not occur during mid-life but during the first stressful years of the relationship. In one study the level of sexual satisfaction in mid-life remained much the same, both positive and negative, throughout one's life, and only 2 per cent of married men reported that they had more than one current sexual partner. The so-called 'empty nest' syndrome seems to be a myth as well. Women's lives often take on a new and fulfilling direction when their children leave home, and while there are adjustments to be made from full-time parenting it is not as dramatic as we are led to believe. In fact, family life becomes less demanding in mid-life as the children become more independent while still maintaining links with the family unit. Overall, people in mid-life reported a higher degree of satisfaction with life than those ten years younger, and this contentment seems to increase into late middle age and beyond. A recent survey states that the happiest people in England are married men and single women. These are important facts as they support the authors' point of view that mid-life is a creative and fulfilling time, more typified by satisfaction and new challenge than by depression and loss.

Let us return to Amanda who was mourning her loss of youth and beauty at the beginning of the chapter. She is an interesting woman because, as mentioned before, her life has been a series of struggles and losses balanced by her seeking out counselling to obtain a caring, but emotionally uninvolved, reflection of her process. Amanda is unusual in that she has been willing to face both her real and imagined losses and attempt to put them in perspective in the entirety of her life experience. There has been some quite real pain in her life. She made a glamorous marriage to an Australian author and their sexual life was an important component of that glamour. Judging from the photographs she still carries with her, they made a stunning couple in the swinging London of the 1960s, and they were at the centre of a cosmopolitan set who crossed between the worlds of art and academia. Amanda and her husband built a life and family based around their shared interests, and she now says that she finds it hard to believe how arrogant they quickly became. 'It all came so easy, and I couldn't understand why everyone wasn't able to have a flat in Hampstead, a career and children, foreign holidays and lots of interesting friends. I don't think we ever consciously looked for these things; they just were . . . they were our life.' The confidence given to them both by their success, attractiveness and achievements did not encourage them towards introspection, and it was with this attitude they moved without noticing into their thirties.

> As I grew older I slowly began to realize that I wouldn't be young forever, and at the same time I began to realize how important being beautiful and successful were to me. My husband moved to more complex work and was in more and more demand for his maturity. I began not to be the most beautiful woman in the room, and I was shocked how important that was to me. I felt like a vain fool when this part of myself was revealed. I think this is what brought me to counselling the first time . . . the shame I felt about fearing the loss of my beauty. I can laugh about it now . . . well, sort of.

Amanda's mid-life negotiation began when the façade of the life she and her husband had constructed began to peel and then to crumble. The couple who had everything began to realize that they had colluded to create a false image for the world and for themselves. At the same time Amanda was feeling uneasy about her fading beauty, she learned that her husband had been unfaithful to her, and this discovery was even more damaging for her as his relationships outside the marriage were with men. This discovery made her doubt her ability to hold her husband as her youth disappeared and she feared abandonment. Amanda also felt quite strongly that their previous life must have been a lie and that meaning was being robbed from her life. Amanda's story may seem particularly dramatic and it would be quite natural to shower her with sympathy, but she is too courageous to accept that as she acknowledges her own part in the life she and her husband built for fifteen years.

> I married Gordon because I thought I deserved him; he was just as attractive and successful as I was and I never thought about him as a person. We seemed to be the perfect completions to one another's dreams, and of course the outside world gave us lots of support and attention for being together. I don't think we ever

13

had one serious conversation in the first fifteen years of our marriage; there was no need and there was no time. However, I am just as much to blame as Gordon; I needed to believe that he was the perfect match for me and that we had the perfect marriage.

Amanda's life entered a new stage when she turned thirty-five as she faced the problems in her marriage and her own flagging confidence in her ability to compete with younger, more attractive women. She began to feel that her career as a university lecturer was no longer fulfilling and that the university had lost interest in her as she was no longer a young, beautiful, clever academic; something about her uniqueness was fading and Amanda was compelled to look inside herself. What she found there were inner resources which have carried her through some very difficult times. Initially she dealt with the complex dynamic of accepting her beauty and the changing nature of physical attractiveness in a sexist and highly sexualized society. Amanda began to look for the woman under the beautiful mask and what she found was a mixture of insecurity, arrogance, anger and strength. She was able to hold on to all the good things that described her life with Gordon and took great confidence from her success as a mother. Rather than rejecting the importance of her physical appearance, Amanda began to accept that she would be an attractive woman at thirty-five, and forty-five, and on into her fifties and sixties, but in different ways from before. She accepted that this would always be important to her, and that to attempt to cast it away would only bring more pain. Amanda set this aside and held it in balance with her need to continue the relationship with her husband, maintain the family structure, and to re-examine her career goals: 'In therapy I was able to affirm the good things about me and about my life, and in some sense to begin to let go of some of the aspects of my life which caused me pain'.

At the same time Amanda was experiencing what must have been a very disturbing time in her life, she began to feel a need to explore her spiritual life.

Of course, I had been confirmed at school, Gordon and I had a very smart wedding at my parish church in Surrey, and the children had been 'done' when they were babies. Why not, it was

14

an excuse for a great party? But when I was trying to face up to things in my life, I found myself slipping into churches to sit quietly for a few minutes. I work in the City and there are lots of churches, so I was able to visit several each week without being noticed or chatted up by the vicar. It became an important idea for me, especially since it was one of the few times in the week when I could be alone with myself. I didn't really pray; I just let God know how unhappy I was and how angry I had become because I felt he was letting me down. Life in abundance Scripture says, bloody lie I said.

Locating anger somewhere outside one's own situation is quite a common theme in mid-life renegotiation, and God is a convenient abstract father figure as Amanda began to realize.

The change came for me when I made a mistake one lunch time; I was sitting in the small chapel at St Vedast, Foster Lane, just behind St Paul's Cathedral, getting angry at myself, Gordon and God when the small bell rang announcing the lunchtime Euchar-ist, and I was trapped as I could not gracefully slip out as the priest came to the altar. I had never gone in for High Church things, or church things at all for that matter, so I was surprised when I found myself approaching the altar rail to receive com-munion. I am not a mystical person and I have never really been a spiritual person, but I cannot describe the sense of relief and calm I felt after I had sat through what they call mass and received the bread and wine. My anger was still with me but it had been changed somehow . . . perhaps it was incorporated into some-thing greater. At any rate, I became what is known as a regular communicant. Weekday communion got me through some very bad times, and now I go on Sunday to my local church when I can, two or three times a month; I'm not a church person, but it's the least I can do for myself and for God.

Amanda's story is important as she pictures several aspects of the challenges faced by men and women in the middle years. While her situation is unique, and quite glamorous to those of us who live more mundane lives, it contains the elements common to many of our mid-life transitions. The combination of emotional growth and movement towards a mature understanding of herself and her motivations have given Amanda the opportunity to affirm the good and bad about herself. Her conclusion is that she is inherently good and that as she struggles to let go of the pain of the past while holding on to those memories which give her strength she can build a future. In fact, Amanda has struggled for the past twenty-five years as she is now sixty; and her life has changed dramatically in some ways and remained the same in others.

Her marriage is still intact as she found that Gordon was someone she did love and someone whose depth she had never explored; her children are now grown and, after some very stormy adolescent rebellions, they seem to be building stable lives. Her career has taken an unexpected turn. She had spent all her life in education and, as she entered her middle years, Amanda found herself tiring of the round of teaching and writing for publication; she began to look for a way to be more involved with people and less with ideas, facts and abstract thought. Her own experience of counselling led her to do a part-time counselling course, and for the past decade she has worked as a counsellor in a large London teaching hospital where she facilitates staff and student groups as well as working with individual clients. This move to a closer involvement with feelings and the less competitive aspects of one's career is often seen in men and women as they enter mid-life, and it seems to be a natural and healthy direction.

Amanda is not eager to give much credit to her relationship with God for assisting in her mid-life changes, but it is clear even to the casual observer that the discovery of a spiritual depth has played an important role in the second part of her life. The search for meaning in a complex world is assisted by some understanding of one's own feeling about the larger issues of life: death, ageing, the unfairness of much of the events in people's lives, and the issue of pain. While some religious bodies will offer clear-cut solutions through the acceptance of a set of doctrinal assertions, many people look for a more tolerant and integrated spirituality. Fundamentalist Christianity offers seemingly easy answers to these complex problems, but they do not work for everyone. The challenge for people entering mid-life is to find an appropriate means to access the transcendent, the life of the spirit, and each person must decide what that will be. At both levels of her life, the emotional and the spiritual, Amanda did the courageous thing; she listened to what her own inner self was saying.

Mid-life can be a time given to us to pause, to listen and to re-evaluate our lives. Another interesting aspect to Amanda's story is that mid-life change has not been a one-off event for her: like many men and women she has found that she has entered the process several times in the ensuing decades since she turned thirty-five. Many people report that a ten-year cycle is experienced although the subsequent re-evaluations are not as dramatic or as exhausting as the first. These are men and women who are able to hold on to past experience and use it in the future, and this is one of the real gifts of middle age. In relating Amanda's story, we have not touched deeply on her relationship with her husband. Gordon experienced his own mid-life adjustments and his story is recognizable in later chapters.

While mid-life is a time of great change and difficulty for most people, we do not all live such seemingly glamorous existences as did Amanda and Gordon. However, their story does illustrate the richness and potential which the second stage of life holds for us all. This is a time when we are able to abandon the ego-building activities of our first years as much of what we had set out to do has been accomplished. Some men and women fall into the trap of remaining with the sense of emptiness which can come at this time and never move beyond this point. Earlier we described people as saying, 'Is that all there is?' when they had completed the first stage of life, and for some this will be true. They never move through the ennui of partially accomplished goals, for most of us only realize some aspects of our early dreams, and they are not able to set new priorities for themselves. Others can face mid-life by repeating the patterns of the past and setting out to relive another first stage of life. This is quite dangerous since it only postpones the inevitable as at some point these new goals will be completed in some way, and the interior work will still remain to be done.

2

RELATIONSHIPS

Relationships are central to our lives and there is no way that we can escape them. From one point of view life can be seen as a continuous set of interlocking relationships making up a complex matrix which becomes our day-to-day life. If one aspect of mid-life change could be singled out as the most typical beginning point for most men and women in the renegotiation process, it is the reordering of our existing relationships. At this point many people begin to examine their existing family, loving and professional relationships and to adjust them to meet the needs of the next stage of life. This chapter will examine how we choose our partners and build relationships, and the need sometimes to change patterns of relating which no longer meet our needs.

The central relationship in our lives is the partner we choose; and the advent of middle age is often a time when men and women look again at the reasons for the choice. Most people form a significant relationship in their early twenties which usually becomes recognized by the world either in a legal or social sense. What people entering mid-life find is that often their choice of partner was made for reasons which no longer hold true, and the challenge here is deciding how to go on: either alone, in a new relationship, or more hopefully to renew the existing relationship. The difficulty for many people is that early choices were made for a variety of reasons. In our experience many marriages and permanent relationships begin due to social expectations. Women will choose a partner because it seems like the right time to marry and may overlook worrying personality traits. Men are expected to marry, and if a man doesn't marry by the time he is in his early thirties family and friends begin to assume that he is either gay or unable to form positive relationships with women. Most people choose partners from their own social or professional world, and these relationships are often quite fulfilling. However, there are many reasons for choosing a partner, and sexual attraction, social standing, intelligence and convenience are among the less acknowledged motivations. There are three types of permanent relationships which are most useful to examine when beginning a mid-life renegotiation since many people fall into one of the three types or a mixture of them.

It is quite typical of relationships formed in the very early twenties, or even late teenage years, for the partners to use one another and the relationship as a vehicle for growing up together. This can be extremely fulfilling if the partners allow one another to grow at their own rates, although all too often one partner will leap ahead leaving the other feeling inadequate and immature. We find it is often the men in these type of partnerships, who through their professional lives grow more quickly especially if the woman gives up her working life to raise a family. The daily round of childrearing, managing the household and meeting a working husband's emotional needs can rob a woman of the time and space she needs for her own growth. Anger, resentment and depression are common outcomes of this scenario. At mid-life a sensitive man can begin to tap his own creative energies by allowing his partner to explore new avenues while he begins to learn more about the world of feelings. Partners in a relationship formed early on in life have a special bond and a special responsibility to one another as they approach mid-life. There is so much depth, history and time invested in these types of partnerships that the potential for growth can be an exciting prospect.

Another type of permanent relationship which is quite common is the healing relationship. This can take the form of mutual healing or one partner providing the healing environment for the other. This is an aspect of all good relationships and couples undergoing change need to look to one another before rushing to an ending. There can be tremendous dangers in these types of relationships but also the potential for a deep sharing of love and understood pain which is unique. A sad but beautiful relationship which was mutually healing is revealed in the story

19

of David and Diane who met and married while they were in their twenties. Both partners had been raised in extremely conservative fundamentalist Christian families which emphasized a judgemental and behaviour-oriented view of human life: God set down laws for humanity which were to be obeyed strictly and without question. David was destined for ministry in his small sect but was able to break away while attending the church's training college. His first marriage to a woman he met within the sect ended quite quickly and he moved into a highly paid job as a research chemist. Diane alternately rebelled against and conformed to her family's expectations, but never was able to form a permanent relationship with a man in reaction to her strict, authoritarian father.

When she and David met as adults they recognized the pain inside one another and were able to reach out to form an environment where they could begin to heal the wounds. Their sexual relationship was a major element in this healing process, and this became the basis for forming deeper bonds of trust and shared knowledge of one anothers' past deprivation. The healing process took the form of enabling the other to try avenues of expression which they had never dared before. David was able to leave the security of his job to begin life again as a craftsman with Diane's support and love. Diane channelled her creative energies into her nursing career which became renewed when she married David. Their relationship was not without a high level of emotional testing of one another as both had been so hurt in the past. They worked to accept their families within the context of their love and found that they could build new bridges to them. In some way the pain they shared bonded them even more closely and as the relationship endured for many years and their level of trust deepened they became a dynamic and successful couple. David's new career burgeoned and he found a new sense of self-worth through working with his hands, creating beautiful objects. Everyone around them acknowledged that theirs was a unique relationship which took its power from mutual healing.

Unfortunately David died quite suddenly in a car accident and five years on Diane is still attempting to come to terms with the pain. However, part of this new healing process for her is acknowledging what they were able to give to one another during the decade they were together. It was a place of healing, but could the relationship have survived? So much energy was put into the partnership that there was no room for children, and it was clearly a 'hothouse' relationship that might have not survived a mid-life change.

A third type of relationship formed in early life is the one in which one partner asks too much of the other or one partner is willing to give more than is appropriate. A telling example of the dangers inherent in these relationships is shown by Amy who unconsciously chose her husband while at university so she could be healed of early parental deprivation; however, the choice contained great dangers for her.

> I could never understand why he wanted me; I felt surrounded by his love and care, and for the first time in my life I felt wanted and valued. He was not put off by my depression or sexual frigidity and would spend hours encouraging me to talk and to share my feelings with him. I didn't love him; I didn't know what love was but he seemed so sure that I was the one special person for him, so we married. I realize now that a disabling pattern was set from the very beginning. I would get depressed and frightened, he would take care of me, I would feel demeaned by the rescuing but could not tell him so because I did not want to hurt him. I wanted to leave several times, but I thought that would be too cruel, so I stayed to continue the pattern for almost fifteen years. We never moved on; he was wasting his life trying to heal me in a vain hope that he could heal himself; of course he never admitted that he had any problems. Only when we entered middle age did I begin to find the courage to ask for more independence to deal with my own feelings in my own way. It destroyed our marriage and gave me back my life.

Amy's story clearly illustrates the dangers inherent in relationships where one partner either asks too much of the other or is willing to give too much for his or her own reasons.

So far the discussion has focused upon relationships which take the form of marriage, and marriage will be looked at in further depth in this chapter, but there are many types of important relationships other than marriage which make up our lives. Friendship is often overlooked when discussing mid-life, but these associations can often be more important and more enduring than marriages. An important area often overlooked is friendship between men and women which does not include sexual content. Relationships within families often provide an important sense of continuity in our lives and are particularly important for single people. Relationships which have spiritual content or bonding also become more important in mid-life. These frequently are between minister or priest and parishioner, with a spiritual director or friend, and with members of a congregation who share a specific faith tradition. One of the difficulties in our society is that we are hesitant to speak about sex, and there is an even greater taboo when speaking about sexual relationships. It is acceptable to allude to the sexual content within marriage or to discuss a sexual affair with a friend, but there is little serious discussion of the role sexuality plays in our relationships, whether it is expressed physically or not. However, let us begin a more detailed examination of relationships with marriage and bonded stable relationships.

In mid-life marriages do not end with the frequency that we are led to believe; however, they do change at this time more than at any other. Mid-life can be a time for asking important questions and searching for the appropriate answers: 'Do I still want this person?', 'What is there about this marriage that is worth saving?', 'Who is this person I live with?' When the partners in a marriage enter mid-life it can be a time for renegotiating the contract formed early on. The decision at this time is either to replace the relationship with another or to refurbish it with a new, mutually agreeable contract. It is naive to think that relationships which are expected to endure for a lifetime can remain the same. Real relationships are based on a desire to share life's journey with another. As our journey changes and develops so should our marriage contracts. The man who has spent years earning the money for the family can request a job or career change which may reduce the family's standard of living but improve its quality of life. The woman who has been out at work may be able to choose to take a few years off and pursue her own personal goals.

If marriages are to remain mutually fulfilling then there is a need to re-examine each partner's needs on a regular basis. As we live longer relationships can last longer, and the challenge is to make them work over a longer period of time. There can be a sense of panic in mid-life when partners look at the past fifteen years and realize that they may well have to spend another twenty or thirty years together. Is this what they meant when they took one another for better or worse, or can marriage become a creative and dynamic process rather than a binding contract fixed at a time when needs were different? The successful mid-life marriage is described by its ability to tolerate growth and exploration on the part of both parties. Sometimes this can take the simple form of a role reversal for a period of time, a not uncommon practice in this climate of enforced redundancy. Surprisingly to some, many men welcome the idea of staying at home for a period of time to deal with teenage children, household management, and the variety of small tasks which take up time spent in daily living.

Another area not often discussed in marriage is sexuality, particularly infidelity and loss of sexual excitement. However, these are concerns which are quite commonly brought to counsellors. How marriage partners deal with infidelity is often a sign of the stability of their relationship. There are few people who are not hurt when their partner chooses to have a sexual affair outside of their relationship and that must be acknowledged. Infidelity can be a catalyst for change and renegotiation or a means of expressing anger and punishment by both parties. As we have cited earlier, most middle-aged men are not having sexual affairs – less than 2 per cent according to one study – and, of course, women do have affairs as well. The important thing to consider for our discussion is the role these affairs may play in mid-life change. It is important to ask oneself why the affair started and what need it is fulfilling. Often there is a loss of sexual excitement in long-term relationships, and that is an inherent problem. There is a growing industry in sexual advice and everyone is aware of sex advisers in the media recommending exotic techniques to keep the excitement level high in a marriage. This approach was mocked quite tellingly recently in the film *Fried Green Tomatoes at the Whistle Stop Café* where the wife answered the door to her

23

husband wearing cling film and nothing else! The sad lesson here is that it was a desperate attempt to reach out to her partner who no longer saw her as a person. In reality, some of the answers to maintaining sexual excitement in a marriage are quite mundane but often overlooked. What we all want as a person, and as a sexual being, is to be valued. Making time for sex, remembering to bathe, wearing pleasant smelling perfume or aftershave, concentrating on sharing pleasure with your partner rather than looking for orgasm, are all common sense, and we don't need a sex manual to remember these. Again, mid-life is often a time of setting new priorities and putting one's own needs out in the open for discussion. A big step towards renewing sexual excitement in a marriage is admitting to one another that the excitement is gone or fading. Once that is admitted openly, then the tension is broken and beginnings towards a renewal of excitement can begin.

The last aspect of mid-life marriage to be considered is the area of competitiveness in careers. This is something of a new phenomenon in the postwar period as more and more women have started careers of their own. The Feminist Movement of the last twenty years has slowly made an impact in professions which were previously male dominated. Mid-life is a dangerous time professionally for both men and women. It is in the late thirties that senior promotions are made and if one partner passes another difficulties can occur. Another common scenario is for a wife to return to work and find herself more successful than her husband. There is no easy answer to this problem, and certainly the answer is not for the woman to give up her career to make her husband feel better. In mid-life it is appropriate for us all to examine our careers and decide how we feel about continuing on the track we have taken. How important is promotion, influencing policy, or making a large salary? Many people find that these goals were set in our early years and no longer reflect our feelings about work. Perhaps mid-life can be a time to relax career goals and to pursue other interests concurrently. Another approach is for one partner to step back from the fast track in their career and take on more responsibility for the relationship while the other moves on. Of course, it is also possible to change the structure of

24

the relationship by bringing in outside help to manage the home so both partners can continue a strong work commitment.

In the past few years there has been a trend towards the affirmation of marriage as the only model for committed relationships between men and women. There has been much emphasis on the family unit from both the Government and Church, and this furthers the feelings of isolation by those living in non-traditional relationships, especially gay men and lesbians. The truth is that a large majority of our population live in relationships which do not involve marriage; this includes both heterosexual and homosexual men and women. The attitude of the mainline churches is one of quiet tolerance, but these institutions withhold their approval or even open discussion of the problems inherent in gay and lesbian relationships. At some level this lack of support is bound to contribute to the breakdown of committed same-sex relationships. However, it must be said that there are a great many of these partnerships which endure for many years and even lifetimes. Gay men and lesbians face special concerns in mid-life, and they often have little opportunity for exploration and support when they enter middle age. Some counsellors still do not recognize same-sex relationships as valid and even maintain that homosexuality is an emotional dysfunction, if not a mental illness. It is still a fact that it is not possible for openly gay men or lesbians to become fully qualified psychoanalysts in the major British training programmes because of this reason.

When gay men and lesbians reach the mid-life stage many have spent years attempting to build lasting relationships despite the prejudice and lack of support from society. Much of their personal lives is split off from their professional lives as it is still not acceptable to talk about one's same-sex partner in most workplaces, let alone bring them along to social gatherings. Gay men and lesbians are often seen as aloof and distant by their co-workers and much of this must come from their quite understandable reticence to speak about the other parts of their lives in a relaxed manner.

The following dialogue between two gay men who came for counselling reveals many of the problems faced in same-sex relationships as they enter mid-life renegotiation. Bob is forty-four and his partner Jamie is thirty-two, both have successful careers and their relationship has endured for ten years. They came to counselling because Bob wants to return to the United States where he grew up, and Jamie was at a point in his life where he was being offered a major promotion in his work. Moving would mean starting all over again and this had serious implications for the continuance of the partnership. Other issues arise in the passage including the threat of AIDS, the fear of the loss of youth, the prejudice of Church and society, and the frustration at having no place in which to discuss these issues. It is also interesting to notice the self-depreciating humour used by the two men to describe themselves and other gay men which is a good reflection of how society feels about them. The humour is a defence against the negative attitude towards gay relationships in our society and the lack of support which these partnerships receive. The humour masks the pain of always living a life on the margins of heterosexual society.

Jamie I think it's pathetic that we're here. It's not fair that we have to pay for counselling when other people just talk about this stuff at work or with their family or priest . . . or almost anywhere.

Bob Yeah, sure . . . you just see us going to Fr Euen with this stuff, he's a 'no hoper'.

Counsellor Your priest wouldn't accept you as a couple?

(*Both men turn to one another and exchange smiles.*)

Bob We would get a pious homily about friendship. He'd dodge the issues and I'd just come away feeling angry. It's useless.

Jamie Tell the truth, Bob. Fr Euen is gay but he'd never admit it. He's even got a boyfriend; the lovely Frank. But, you know, they're just good friends . . . wink, wink, nudge, nudge. He's worse off than we are; he can't even admit to himself that he's gay; he just keeps that part of himself hidden away. I can't blame him in one way; the parish would not think it is a charming idea to have a poofter for a priest.

Bob Euen's got his own problems alright, but that's not why I'm here. He can find his own counsellor, not that he ever will. I'll make a start because this is costing us money. Jamie and I have been together for almost ten years, but as they say, 'it ain't been easy'. At first it was true love, or true sex I should say; but then when we decided this was a big time romance things started getting a bit more complicated. We finally decided to live together, then we started sharing money, and then it just seemed that this was the way it had always been. I'm 'out' at work, but Jamie is not, so at least I can talk about him with some of my colleagues. When he feels like it he comes along to parties and things, but he's got his own life to live . . . he's not my wife.

(*They look at one another and laugh again.*)

Jamie Hardly . . . might be the other way around most of the time. (*Bob blushes and moves in his chair.*) Like Bob says, it hasn't been easy, but we've made a life for ourselves. We seem to be drifting and now Bob wants to go off to the States and we'd have to start all over again. So we have to decide whether we go, or whether I don't go, or whether we both don't go. If I go that means that I start all over again at the bottom of the nursing ladder just when I'm in line for a management post which would mean a lot more money and a lot more responsibility. But I don't even know if that's what I want; in fact, since we're here I'll say that I don't even know if I want to be a nurse any more. I chose it because it was something gay men did and I like taking care of people. I spent enough time taking care of my family that's for sure. Now, I'm a bit fed up with it all . . . it might be nice for someone to take care of me for a while.

Bob I know what Jamie's going through; I felt that way when I was his age and it's OK with me if he wants to make a big change. He could do that in the States for that matter; it might be the right time and place. I left my teaching job when I was his age; in fact it was when we were first together. I got fed up with being so careful with the kids because I'm gay and people might get the wrong idea. I am not attracted to kids, but there's a lot of prejudice around about child molesters (who are almost always straight men). So I took a sideways step into fund raising for an educational trust, but this time I made sure everyone knew I was gay soon after I took on the job. No more closet for me, and maybe I don't make as much money as I could but at least I feel more comfortable with what I'm doing. I feel that this has really helped our relationship because I'm more comfortable with myself now.

Jamie Yeah, that would be one of the good things about the States; I have this fantasy that it would be better there for us as a couple. People might be more supportive and Bob's family in New York knows about us and even likes me . . . well, sort of. This relationship is important to me and I don't want it to end. We're lucky; we're alive at least. Lots of Bob's friends are HIV positive or have AIDS and I don't know how many of our friends here and in the States have died. Someone said that going to memorial services for friends who have died is as common for gay men as going to brunch. I couldn't face trying to put together another relationship like ours and I couldn't go back on the scene again.

Bob It'd be a lot easier for you than me; at least you still have your youthful beauty and charm. If I don't go to the gym at least three times a week all this will expand and slide and soon it will be Mr Blobby, not slim, lithe, boyish Bob. Nobody loves an old poofter . . . especially not other old poofters. What I really mean is that it isn't easy getting old when you're gay; I don't really see myself as old yet, but I have to face the fact that I'm quickly sliding through middle age . . . and it doesn't help that Jamie is ten years younger . . . and I have to admit that I worry that Jamie might want to find someone his own age.

(*Jamie reaches over and puts his hand on Bob's knee.*)

Jamie Hardly . . . you know grey has always been my favourite colour.

This dialogue gives us some insight into the kind of problems faced by gay couples and couples where age difference is a factor. The interesting thing for people without much experience of gay men is that it reveals the issues in the relationship are much like those for heterosexual couples. Of course, children are not usually an issue, which gives many same-sex couples more freedom to negotiate the mid-life period, but the most poignant aspect of these types of relationships is the lack of support, both from the gay community and society as a whole, that gay men and women feel.

Children, however, are a big issue for most couples, and the place of children and family life is very important when people reach mid-life. In the past twenty years it has been a growing trend for couples to put off having children until well into their thirties, if at all. This has the effect, in our experience, of lengthening the first stage of life where men and women focus on specific goals set by them under influences from family and society. They find it much easier to maintain two career relationships without children, and decisions about relocating, changing jobs and working long hours are not as complex when there are no children. This delaying of beginning a family can lead to a panic in mid-life with concerns about leaving it all too late. As couples sail comfortably through their twenties and thirties building a lifestyle characterized by freedom and a good deal of material goods the thought of complicating life with children becomes sharp. For women the societal pressure to have children is great, and women who do choose to have both career and family are often accused of wanting too much or wanting it all. The decision to have children can often spark off a mid-life change as it has deep ramifications for the couple. Many couples come to counselling over this issue, and it is even more difficult for Christian couples as the family is held in high esteem: couples without children do not easily fit into congregations and there is a feeling of suspicion about them. Deciding to have children for couples who have waited or who are barren and who are considering adoption brings into focus issues about the relationship and the changes to be faced.

Most parents know how much a child changes the dynamics, both emotional and sexual, and some relationships are not strong enough to bear this. When the decision is faced the feelings, both positive and negative, can be quite powerful, and can call into question the nature of the relationship. Will the relationship work with children? Who takes the responsibility for the childcare? Why are children wanted? These are all complex questions and ones which must be worked out within the context of what has gone before for the couple and what is to come. As in many mid-life negotiations the decisions reached often contain a surprising amount of compromise on the part of both partners, and many mid-life men eagerly accept the role of co-parent. In many ways, men may well be more ready for the change as they have achieved career goals with varying degrees of success and may want to concentrate on developing their feeling and caring side. Women, on the other hand, often fear that adding children to a relationship will mean an extra load of emotional and physical responsibilities which they will be expected to carry. Sadly, this is usually the reality when children enter a family dynamic.

The role of children in relationships is always a complex one, and one which in the early years many parents take for granted. Only at mid-life do many parents begin to realize how much their children have become projections of their own expectations and dreams. The frustrated musician sees his son on the concert stage, the woman who was not popular at school encourages her daughter to make herself a social success while playing down academic pursuits, working-class couples want higher education for their children which was denied to them by circumstance, and middle-class couples want a private education which their parents were not able to afford. In mid-life many parents find their children gaining a sense of their own identity and rejecting the scenarios offered to them by their parents. This is often emotionally destructive as parents see themselves and their children as failures, and a mid-life examination often ensues. This brings up the problem of when to let go of our children and how to do so. In mid-life it is common for children in most families to be at the age when they are leaving school or home for higher education. Couples can feel an emptiness in the relationship as they go through the difficult process of deciding how much freedom to give their teenage children. Parenting is an emotionally consuming job and one which can define our self-image; when children leave home or struggle for more independence our own self-image is brought into question. Who are we when we are no longer parents? Children give meaning to our lives and connect us in a metaphysical way with the future; in one sense they are the only lasting contribution to the world as our career accomplishments will soon be forgotten, often soon after retirement. This brings many parents to what can be seen as an existential crisis in mid-life which is responsible for much of the ennui or loss of meaning in life which people experience at this time. For men, it can be quite acute but not acknowledged and they will focus on other issues while masking the true existential one. These feelings can be transferred to worries about their job, redundancy, or loss of sexual potency.

It is not an uncommon scenario for parents to be quite threatened by their children's sexuality, especially if it deviates from their own. Sexually active young people bring great difficulties into families where sex is not openly discussed, and a young person's active sexual life can call into question the parents' own sexual life. If they have experienced a loss of sexual excitement in their relationship, and most couples who are together for very long do, this can be even more painful. The vigour and potential for life which children bring to a relationship can be invigorating and debilitating at the same time. As they grow stronger, sexually active, academically and professionally successful, our own accomplishments in these areas are called into question. Much of the disturbances in families at mid-life can be attributed to the difficult problem of accepting our children's entry into the adult world, but this is not often acknowledged. Accepting this ourselves is the first step, and can lead to an open discussion with one's children which then often leads to a great release of pressure in the family. One of the first and most important tasks for mid-life parents is this acceptance; when it occurs it is much easier to proceed with a positive renegotiation towards a renewed life with the children.

Parenting is a complex task and one at which not everyone is successful. While it is easy to blame all the problems of a child on its parents, this is not always useful. All young people go through a stage where they feel that their parents have made major mistakes in their upbringing; this is quite natural and parents should accept this as a normal part of the parenting process. However, it is true that some parents are not good enough for a variety of reasons: they may have emotional problems of their own or were too young to take on the responsibilities of a child. In our experience of group therapy with university students, the main

31

complaint about parents is emotional distance. It may be phrased in a variety of ways in counselling sessions, but what these young people mean is that for whatever reason their parents did not enter their lives positively and accept them as individuals. When this is combined with a strict, authoritarian family structure, real damage can be done to children. The task for mid-life parents who feel that they have failed their children in some way is to examine their parenting roles and to question if they were emotionally present for their children. While it is possible to reclaim a relationship with an adult or teenage child, it is not possible to make up for past mistakes. What can be done is to acknowledge them and to work with one's children to make a future where they are given the love and support they deserve. This can be one of the most rewarding accomplishments of mid-life renegotiation as it can give us back children that we may feel we have lost, thereby reconnecting us existentially with the future.

While mid-life parents may be negotiating their future with their children they are strongly linked to their own past history in the form of their own parents. As our own parents age new demands for care and oversight may be placed upon us. It is easy to view this as a burden which comes at a difficult time in our lives, but there is great potential for growth here as well. The issues brought up by ageing parents centre around our own experience as children, and one of the most common problems faced in mid-life is that of becoming the parent to one's own parents. After establishing ourselves in our careers and personal relationships, it can be a difficult situation to be called to return to closer contact with parents from whom one has successfully separated. Society and the Church tell us that it is our responsibility and one that should be taken with joy, but that is rarely the case. Our parents almost inevitably see us as children and the relationships can founder as parents reluctantly become more and more dependent on the child. In mid-life the sense of being trapped is often heightened by these new responsibilities, and it is important that a sense of independence is maintained for as long as possible. While taking ageing parents into one's own home is common in traditional societies, today's complex lifestyles do not always make this possible or desirable. Mid-life can be a time for sorting out our past relationship with our parents, especially if it has been bad. Given the wisdom of experience, it is possible for ageing parents and children to forgive one another for past mistakes and pain and to renew their relationships. We feel that this must be done at some point in everyone's lives, and unfortunately most people leave it until it is too late. The death-bed of a parent is not the place to heal a lifetime of anger and frustration, and what is even more common is years of therapy after a parent dies. The most important thing to keep in mind when dealing with parental issues is that the past can be redeemed, but it cannot be changed. Pain from childhood stays with us and cannot be erased by counselling or prayer; what can be done, however, is working towards an acceptance of the past, negotiating some kind of inner forgiveness, and accepting that all that has gone before contributes towards the person we are today.

Both authors have lost parents; our experience is not unique, but Alvin's is typical of what many men face when their father dies. His experience is summarized in the answer to the often asked question, 'What made you go back into therapy at forty-seven?'

My father died early in the year that I returned to therapy. I flew home to do the funeral which I now realize was a mistake – not going home, but doing the funeral for my family. I was robbed of my own grief as I had to carry the communal pain, anger and sense of existential loss for my large family. It is interesting that I did not question the 'rightness' of my doing the funeral when they asked; it's a pattern for me always to be there for people. I was working as a curate in the East End at the time and for months after I found myself standing at my study windows overlooking Shandy Park staring off into the plane trees each afternoon. I was overcome by a great sense of emptiness and sadness about life, especially when I would watch the children at play in the park below. My vicar, who had lost his own father a year earlier, told me to take my time and not to be surprised when the sadness didn't leave immediately. Good words but I didn't believe him because I had never been close with my emotionally distant Swiss father. I was like a stranger to him, a visitor from another planet with my academic and intellectual accomplishments. I thought that I must be going through yet another mid-life negotiation as life seemed without meaning and I was plagued by sleepless nights and afternoons when I couldn't tear myself away from the study windows. I didn't relate it to my father's death.

This continued for several months; I lost weight, started smoking again, stopped eating, became listless and couldn't bring myself to do my parish duties. One morning I was dressing after my shower and turned as I pulled on my jeans to look at myself in the mirror. What I saw was my father as I had last seen him before he died: an emaciated, balding grey man whose skin hung in slack bunches on his large frame . . . eyes that seemed huge and staring due to the weight loss but without lustre or life. I experienced a tremendous sense of loneliness and isolation in a global way . . . that I was now alone forever in this frightening world. I sat on the edge of the bed half dressed, very much in touch with the little boy that is never too far from the surface and cried for myself and the father I barely knew. Then I rang a friend who is a priest and a psychotherapist and asked for a referral, and this began my most current mid-life renegotiation.

What is most telling about this story is the feeling that most of us share when we lose a parent, even a parent with whom we have not been close, that we are now alone in the world. The grief is compounded by the realization that even the possibility for that closeness is finished. It is often said that we never really consider ourselves adult until our parents die, and this is true. However, the deeper truth is the sense of aloneness which usually accompanies this transition and the fear that comes with it. Important and global questions about the meaning of life, our choices, and our future are called into consideration and are often the beginning of a mid-life renegotiation. For Alvin the working through of these problems took the form of psychotherapy and spiritual direction as the spiritual issues are as important as the emotional ones. From our point of view, one cannot take place without the other, and the danger is that many people feel counselling can be seen as a medical model for renewing emotional health. A good dose of counselling and you're on your way again. Let's return to Alvin talking about his spiritual direction which ran concurrently with his therapy.

My spiritual director is a lovely man; he did my ordination retreat and I've been going to him on a regular basis for almost eight years now. He is about ten years older than me and comes from the same spiritual tradition, catholic, so he knows how I feel about the sacraments, my priesthood, and all that stuff. We talk about many of the same things as I talk about with my therapist but from a different perspective. He constantly asks me where God is in it for me. I have to stop and think about that each time it comes up and this keeps me from feeling that my intellectual process is the most important way of looking at things. As a Christian it's important for me to see how God is working in my life and it is too easy to slip into a psychotherapeutic omnipotence where I feel that if I can just get it sorted out in my mind everything will fall into place. I'm very lucky in that he never offers answers, only suggestions for deepening and speaking with God. I think he knows that God will do the work with me if I just let him. That's it really; somehow my spiritual director is one of the agents through which I am able to access my spiritual life . . . does that sound too cosmic or pretentious? If it does, I guess it's because I have a tendency to be that way. What I do know is that I need both points of view or I'd be left wallowing in my own sadness and sense of loss.

The relationship between spiritual director and directee is one of the unique types of friendship open to us all. However, most men and women have a variety of types of friendships which sustain them in life. We find that friends often fall into two categories: those who enable us and those we care for. Most of us have friends of both types and if the balance is kept somewhat equal both are of use to us. By taking care of friends, listening to their woes and giving advice when asked, sharing common experiences and trading insights, we are given a sense of feeling needed and of being useful. Much of our sense of personal worth can be centred in our friendships, and we value most highly those friends who enable us. The development and nurturing of friendship is not an easy task as so many responsibilities seduce us away from maintaining them. Sometimes our partners resent outside friendships because they feel threatened by the intimacy, but everyone should seek out and develop real friends. Companionship is an important need and relationships can be strengthened by the support that each partner finds in outside friends. However, it must be said that friendships need to be nurtured in much the same way as marriages; it takes time and commitment to keep up with a friend whose life is different from yours. The hard work needed is repaid many times when you know that there is someone outside your everyday life who cares and will understand.

Relationships between women are the most acceptable and the most common in our society. Perhaps the reason for this is that these friendships are safe in society's eyes, and this most certainly contributes to the deep sharing of feelings between women. All the women we have worked with over the years seem to share a similar feeling when they talk about their relationships with other women, namely that these friendships are very different from the relationships between men. They all agree that women are more likely to share feelings with one another, whereas this is just the thing that men complain that they do not have the opportunity or courage to do. Traditionally, the world of emotions has been the main arena in which women are allowed to express themselves without restraint. This has both positive and negative implications for their lives, but it is often used against them in male-female relationships and in the workplace. While women agree that they are more free to express their emotions, they report that they have only one or two friends with whom they would share without reservation. Few men would be able to say the same thing as this sharing usually involves failures and weaknesses as well as joy and accomplishments.

Continuing the contrast with men, women feel that they put more time and energy into maintaining their relationships and that these friendships do not have to revolve around doing activities together. It is quite common for men to use a sport or hobby activity as a vehicle to carry the relationship and to justify the

36

time spent together. On the other hand, women will often choose to spend time together for no other reason than wanting to talk and to share their lives; an excuse is not needed. In mid-life these friendships become particularly important as they present a means for exploring the losses and changes to be faced. The advantage for women is that these relationships already exist and often exist with emotional sharing at a deep level, and this gives the confidence of a history of being open and vulnerable at a time when it is particularly important to have support.

Perhaps some of the most difficult types of friendships to maintain are those between men. Men are often quite defended emotionally, and it is not common for men to share their dreams, desires and insecurities with one another after they leave adolescence. However, the growing men's movement with its sometimes silly rituals for male bonding speaks of the deep need men have to be with and to share with one another. Traditionally men will share hobbies, sports, gardening, or DIY projects, but it is rare for men to share their inner feelings. The authors have worked with countless numbers of men who express this desire, but also a fear of what they want at deep level. 'If I come too close to another man will I be mistaken for a homosexual?', 'If I share too much of what's inside me then will I be embarrassed or under his power?', 'How do I begin to deepen my male friendships?' are all questions which come up when men consider closer relationships with other men. Issues of competition, intimacy, and the fear of being misunderstood often prevent men from coming closer to one another. The possibility is there but it takes courage and confidence which men often do not find within themselves and is not fostered by society or the Church. Christian men are encouraged to relate at a deep spiritual level but this is often split off from the rest of their lives. The Church can set unrealistic scenarios for men, and many men complain that the Church wants to feminize them in the sense that they are encouraged to be sensitive and caring by accepting a female model for this. There is a desire among Christian men to search for appropriate male models for relationship, but there seems to be little opportunity for this. A clear example of how uncomfortable men feel with what the Church has to offer can be seen any Sunday during the Peace. The hugging which is encouraged in many charismatic congregations makes most men uncomfortable and has the opposite result intended. Perhaps churches should look towards men's groups which might explore issues of interest and importance to men without the fear of being accused of being sexist or elitist. It is interesting that one of the most moribund male-dominated institutions in Western society provides almost no arena in which men can meet as equals. The most common complaint among mid-life men is not failing sexuality or job dissatisfaction but rather loneliness. It is a sad note that time and again the authors have heard the stories of successful, competent men, which reveal their loneliness and desire for an intimacy and sharing which they do not find in their marriages or at the sports ground.

A happier scenario is the possibility of relationships between men and women who are not sexual or romantic partners. While these friendships can be threatening to partners, the friends report that they are often the long-term sustaining relationships in their lives.

One of the most common, but not often acknowledged, types of friendships is that between gay men and straight (heterosexual) women. These friendships often endure for years and provide each party with unique opportunities for sharing and bonding. Women report that with gay men they are able to share feelings and issues about being a woman and about men in a way they cannot with straight men. The sexual component which often clouds their relationships with straight men is not an issue, and they feel that gay men understand them in a more sensitive way. The feeling that gay men are more sensitive to the emotional needs of women is an important component of these friendships, and women report that gay men can be not only more understanding but more supportive than their husbands or lovers. Of course, some of this may be because they share the common experience of not being straight men in a society which privileges only straight men. There is an unspoken bond which the oppressed share and which makes them feel they can understand one another. Gay men feel that straight women are less judgemental than lesbians and that they understand relationships with men in a way that is useful to them. In mid-life the important aspect of these friendships is the longevity and the support offered to one another during what can be a difficult mid-life adjustment. One such friendship is that of Julian and Carol, two teachers who met when they both worked at a large London comprehensive school in the 1970s. Julian and Carol have been friends for over twenty years and each agreed to respond to the school-essay type question, 'Describe your best friend'. The result makes interesting reading.

My best friend is Carol; we met twenty-three years ago when I took a teaching job at the school where she was working. There's been a lot of water under the bridge since then. However, we are always there for one another; I know that sounds like bad Hollywood dialogue, but it's true. We met the first day of my new teaching job and I loved her sense of humour . . . she was also the first one to show me where my post box was located in the staff room and that's worth a lifetime's friendship on its own! She had this bad pattern of falling in love with married or unavailable men. I knew she fancied me a bit because I'm a fancy-able guy, but since I'm gay it never went anywhere. We shared a lot at school and started doing things outside as well and found that we had the same sort of ironic, but caring, way of dealing with students and our colleagues. She married a mutual friend whom I like . . . most of the time. However, he never worries when we're together or hassles her about the time we spend together. I can say anything to Carol and she accepts what I'm feeling. She doesn't always agree and she's not afraid to give her opinion, but she doesn't boss me around or judge me. I guess you could say this has been a twenty-year love affair without sex. She always remembers my birthday, buys me really great presents because she knows me so well. When I come to visit we always find time to do something special together without our partners, like a boozy lunch followed by indiscriminate shopping. Carol's not a Christian and is a little threatened by my spirituality although she sends her daughter along to Sunday School sometimes. She says that she feels guilty that she has almost no interest in spiritual matters, but then she keeps bringing it up so I wonder. We have similar tastes in books, films and plays which form a big part of what we like about one another. When I told her I was gay she just said that she had thought I was working towards accepting that for a long time. Thank God she didn't ask me if I was sure or if it was just a reaction to failed relationships with women. She knows me too well; sometimes better than I know myself. If I fancied women she would be at the top of my list. I have this fantasy that in old age when our partners die or abandon us that we take a house together and spend the rest of our lives reading books, eating too much rich food, and going out to dinner and theatre every other night . . . and sleeping in the same bed because everyone needs a cuddle now and then. Lots of people and events have come and gone in my life, but Carol is one of several constants; I don't really think I would want to do without her.

My best friend is Julian; we met through work because we taught at the same school for many years. We became friends almost immediately and have stayed so for a long time. I liked his sense of humour and his confidence with teaching; he's very bright and creative in the classroom, and students love him. We did some team teaching together and that was great; we really clicked. Our weak and strong points seemed to make more than one whole teacher; I think the kids were getting the best of both of us. I've always liked Julian's taste and sense of style; he's just as profligate with money as I am and he seems to enjoy life's challenges instead of being punished by them. My husband is not jealous of him and I don't think it's because Julian is gay. We were friends for ten years before he 'came out'. That wasn't easy for me, but I guess I always knew it, and I respect the way he's integrated his life and his responsibilities. Sometimes I think it's easier for me to accept he's gay than it is for me to accept that he's a Christian; it's just not my thing. His partner is OK but I wouldn't say we're friends; I've known Julian from another life and there's probably too much shared past for us to be real friends. I like him, but we are not close. My husband and I visit Julian since he moved far away, and that's always good fun. We seem to slip right back into things like we've never been apart for the last year. He's never lost that cynical but loving sense of humour which I valued so much in him. I'm able to talk to him about my marriage and my job which has changed a lot since he left. I know we'll always be friends and that is more important to me than lots of other relationships. We've been through a lot together, and our friendship makes me feel that there's someone out there who will always understand and accept me. That's money in the bank!

The key relationship for Christians is with God, and this too can change in mid-life. Most of us are raised with a rather traditional model of relationship with God. As young people we are taught that God is the father figure; depending on the faith community, God is sometimes seen as a wise Aryan father, an all-knowing punisher of right and wrong behaviour, or a generalized figure of goodness leading the pack along with the Son and Holy Spirit. In the first stage of life these are often quite useful images as they provide a model against which we can judge our behaviour and accomplishments. As we move into mid-life many men and women feel an emptiness in their relationship with God and this may well be due to an inadequate or immature model of God. Mid-life is often the time when spirituality is embraced in a deeper and broader manner to include one's own life experience when thinking and conceptualizing God. Many people are moving towards seeing God as mother/father, friend, lover, or companion. The authors find the model of God as companion particularly useful for people negotiating mid-life changes. This model removes any judgemental aspect from the relationship; this is not to say, however, that we do not believe in judgement, but that it is an issue of a different order. Seeing God as companion does not remove any of the teachings of traditional Christian theology and, after all, the relationship with God is both private and corporate at the same time. In other words, it is possible to hold flexible and multiple models of God in tension as a Christian.

However, this point of view is often too radical for many mid-life Christians and rather than relaxing and examining their relationship with God, they retreat into reactionary behaviour. It is our experience that it is the mid-lifers who are those who most

41

resist any change in worship, music, or church tradition. It is not surprising that most of those who violently oppose the ordination of women are in this age group, those who beat the Back to Basics and Family Values drum are mid-lifers, and those who make up congregations gathered around one narrow tradition (i.e. 1662 Prayer Book, evangelical fundamentalism, etc.) are in the middle of life. We see this as an often desperate attempt to maintain the status quo in one area while their lives are changing in so many others. On the other hand, it is frequently mid-life women who are the leaven in the spiritual loaf: women have a particular contribution to make in this area as they see God from a feminine perspective and can offer a realistic mature female perspective. Some of the most spiritually centred women in the Church are those in religious orders who have changed with the times and have accepted the challenges of modern life. It is these women who can speak to us about sacrifice, endurance and strength without aggression, as many of them have experienced a lifetime of male oppression in both the Anglican and Roman Catholic communions. We find little anger in these women – something that cannot be said about male priests from both traditions who leave the Church to find themselves in mid-life. The contribution of mid-life women in the areas of spiritual direction, counselling and working with people with HIV / AIDS bears this out.

Mid-life women are also making a new contribution to the work-place. While some men find the trend of women returning to work threatening, the influence they can have on corporate or institutional life can be significant. Mid-life men often see women getting promotion and being hired at mid-management level after years at home as unfair as the men have spent years working to achieve their positions. What they find when they work with and experience mid-life women in the work-place is that they bring with them an ethos of assertiveness and co-operation built on half a lifetime of compromise and negotiation within their families. Although men will acknowledge that they are damaged by aggression, competition and achievement, they find it is difficult to give them up when faced with a woman colleague or manager. It is interesting to note in view of what was said earlier about friendships between gay men and straight women that it is fre-

quently the gay men in a company or institution who will welcome a woman manager or colleague more readily than their
straight counterparts.

If mid-life women are the leaven in the corporate loaf, what is it
that they bring besides an ethos of co-operation? Perhaps the one
most significant contribution they make in the work-place is that,
by their own modelling and experience, the dream of achievement, promotion and success is shown to be a hollow one: women
give mid-life men an opportunity to learn that dreams must be
flexible if they are to be the renewing and refreshing elements in
our lives that we all need. Women transform their dreams and
renew their lives in ways that many mid-life men are not able to
do. The woman who was wife, mother and lover can become the
management trainee, or the woman who at one time climbed
the corporate ladder can step off to have children and become a
work consultant; women seem to be able to do these things without losing a sense of their own personal worth. In our experience,
we find much less depression, if any, among mid-life women
who have been made redundant. There seems to be a power and
resilience there that is, as of yet, untapped by their mid-life male
counterparts.

One of the least talked about and least written about groups of
mid-life men and women are those who are single. This largely
silent group in our society is made up of those who have never
married, those who find themselves without a partner because of
death or divorce, and gay men and lesbians who have not made a
permanent relationship or choose not to do so. The world of
paired people often assumes that single people have a lot to be
thankful for as they do not have the financial or social responsibilities which plague many mid-life couples. However, the fact
that many mid-life singles are quite lonely is more truthful. Often
singles have a close relationship with their parents and when
these parents die in their children's mid-life there is a deep sense
of loneliness and abandonment. When the family home is sold the
last contact with their roots which it symbolized is gone as well,
and it can be a time of frightening desolation. This sense of isolation can combine with other worries at mid-life such as career
plateauing and the lack of children around to maintain a

connection with the future and to give meaning to life. Paired couples find it quite difficult to understand the pain and regret which many mid-life single men and women feel about not having children, and there is a small but growing trend for mid-life women to adopt children.

Marilyn's story highlights many of the fears and problems of mid-life singles. She is a successful health care manager in her early forties who began what she now sees as her mid-life negotiation about five years ago.

> I had some quite serious surgery and was off work for three months and this gave me some time to think and to re-evaluate my life. Both my parents are dead now, and I have nieces and nephews but they live in the South; I only see them at Christmas it seems. I remember lying in bed at home thinking, 'This is nice. My lovely home, my lovely things . . . and they are all paid for. My job is waiting for me when I feel better; I'm a lucky woman. Not many women have the independence and freedom that I do.' Then I began to think about the purpose of all my accomplishments, who would it benefit besides myself and, strangely enough, who would mourn me when I die.

This was the beginning of a life examination which would change Marilyn's future dramatically. After returning to work she found her job less fulfilling than before and each evening when she returned home a mild depression and a deep loneliness settled in. She took the standard advice: bought a cat for company, took up aerobics at her local fitness centre, joined a choir at church and began entertaining friends more regularly. 'It all helped, and my sense of emptiness did diminish, but after a good dose of counselling with a qualified counsellor experienced with women like me I began to understand that what was missing was someone to share my life with. And I came to understand that I did not want a husband or lover, but a child.' Marilyn wanted to exercise her maternal instincts and to share her rich life with another human being, and while the road to adoption has not been easy, it has been possible.

It is easy to accuse someone like Marilyn of selfishness, but from another point of view one of the gifts of singleness is that

one is able to make important life decisions boldly and courageously. In no way would the authors advise single men and
women blindly to follow Marilyn's example, but it is given here to
highlight a variety of options open to singles. The courageous
aspect of Marilyn's decision is not the fact that she chose to adopt
a child, but that she chose to examine her life in middle age and to
change, as she sees it, for the better. We applaud that aspect of her
mid-life process and feel that singles should boldly take up new
challenges in mid-life rather than settling for the status quo, particularly if the status quo is typified by a sense of isolation and
loneliness.

This chapter has examined how in mid-life we are given the
opportunity to reorder relationships formed in the first stage of
life. We have emphasized that choices can and do change, and
that reordering does not usually mean dissolving relationships. If
there is one theme which runs throughout this chapter it has been
that mid-lifers have the opportunity to build on the richness of
what has gone before. Rather than the media image of the mid-life
man or woman throwing off the bonds of the dull past to sail
around the world, find a younger partner, or engage in serial
infidelities we find men and women entering mid-life to be more
thoughtful and presented with more options that might be
believed. The supporting theme of this chapter, the *leitmotif* if you
will, is courage. Mid-life men and women need the courage to
examine the past, to make bold plans for the future and to seek
out emotional and spiritual assistance in doing so. Then the mid-
life adventure can begin.

3

PHYSICAL LOSSES

The scene is a family Christmas Eve party, and near the end of the evening the ubiquitous family photo album comes out. The teenagers in the family gather round to laugh at the funny clothes their parents wore back in the 1960s, and at the baby pictures of themselves surrounded by adoring parents and grandparents. Judy and her two brothers, Paul and David, let out a groan when the page is turned to reveal pictures of their secondary school days. In one Judy, now forty-two, poses in a ballet costume standing on point somewhere in midst of the cast of *The Nutcracker*. 'I'd forgotten all about that; I was a Grand Duchess, but I always wanted to be the Sugar Plum Fairy. In fact, I wanted to be a ballerina; remember all those lessons you two had to take me to? Mum and Dad wouldn't let me go on the tube alone, so one of you had to be my bodyguard. I wonder if I still have my toe shoes?' The plump matron stares for a while at the pencil slim sixteen-year-old in the picture before turning the page. Another groan as her brothers see themselves in running shorts and singlets, arms around one another beaming through their long hair dripping with sweat and full of the pride that only a victory can bring. The boys look almost like twins, slim waisted with tight muscles in their well-defined runners' legs. Paul, a chubby forty-six, says, 'Remember that David? The dynamic duo, half of the county relay championship team. I thought I'd live forever and run forever; now I get out of breath when I have to walk to the corner shop. At least you still run'. David doesn't look pleased. 'If you call it running. At forty-four you're a senior so I'm competing against guys ten years older than me. My knees hurt all the time, if I don't warm up carefully I'll pull a muscle, and I haven't timed myself in months. Too afraid of dropping even more seconds off my mile pace. It's depressing.' A thoughtful silence descends on the three as they remember their youth and it is clear they are wistful about the young people they once were, symbolized by their sporting pictures.

This was an actual scene last Christmas, but it is repeated over and over again in families around the country. We live in a society increasingly obsessed with youth and physical beauty. Images of beautiful young people surround us on advertising hoardings, blonde athletes holding cans of fizzy drink on television commercials, and page after page in the Sunday newspaper supplements advertising skin restoring creams, hair rejuvenation products and exercise equipment – all shown being used by very young and attractive models. How can the middle-aged man or woman cope or compete for attention in this youth-obsessed world? Or perhaps a more apposite question is, how can we accept where we are physically as we enter mid-life?

One of the first signs that we are no longer young is when we find ourselves not able to perform physically at the same level as before. As we enter our thirties it becomes more and more difficult to pretend that we are not ageing, and this realization seems to come hand in hand with the mid-life renegotiation. An acceptance of our changing physical appearance and endurance can even trigger a mid-life examination, especially if we were particularly active in the first stage of life. Even for those of us who did not participate in athletics like the family above, there is no hiding from the fact that we are far past our prime by the time we turn thirty. Physical appearance begins to change, our hair thins, we notice wrinkles and our bodies begin to spread into a softer version of our youthful selves. At the same time our sexual drive begins to change as well; women reach their peak of sexual desire in their early twenties and men much earlier. Since most of us marry then and have children, this realization comes at a time when relationships can experience a diminishing of sexual interest and activity. In fact, some marriages become sexless about this time, and this adds further anxiety to the physical and social pressures we are experiencing. Our stamina is also going through a change as we approach mid-life; it is not so much that we can't do what we've done before, but we cannot do it for as long. In our twenties we could go to the gym on the way to work, spend a day at the office, shop after work before picking up the children, cook and eat a meal, and spend an evening catching up on household chores or socializing; now we find ourselves exhausted at the end of the day and our weekends are spent resting up for the next week.

The fitness centres and gymnasiums across the country are filled with men in their early thirties who are experiencing just what has been described. This is a common reaction to the onset of mid-life, an almost desperate attempt to stave off the inevitable. It is not so much an attempt to regain a lost youth as it is a holding action against the relentless ageing process. For men the importance of body image cannot be over-emphasized. Men appear to define themselves by their own perceptions of body image in either negative or positive ways. Some men may see themselves as weak, soft and unathletic and choose to develop their intellectual powers, but this negative body image still influences their lives quite dramatically. Of course men with a more positive image can suffer emotional stress and trauma when they realize that their once firm, muscular bodies will not always stay that way. For these men a successful mid-life negotiation of one's physical life is very important. This panic at the loss vigour is a very common one: the panic can actually be a healthy step in negotiating the entry into mid-life. Murray, a thirty-six-year-old salesman, started swimming before he began his day's work and was surprised to find himself become part of a group of men of similar age who turned up at his local baths every morning.

It was just the beginning of a lot of changes for me, and I think the panic about my body and my physical appearance led me to reconsider lots of things in my life. It's funny when you think about it; one day I was worrying about my bald spot growing bigger each week and the next my wife and I were having long talks about where our life was going. I'd always been a bit of a lad when it came to sport, played football at school and at college, tennis, swimming, a bit of marathon running when I was younger. In fact, that's how I met Julie, my wife; we were training for the same marathon in the Midlands and she had better times than I did. Then after we got married, the kids arrived and I had less and less time for sport. A couple of years ago from out of the blue after making love, I asked Julie if she still fancied me, still thought I was good looking and sexy. Of course she said yes, but that I wasn't a teenager any longer and that physical appearance becomes less important as we get older. She said she still thought I was a good looking guy, but neither of us were kids any more. Then she said, and I remember this quite clearly, 'Besides, now there's more of you to hold on to'. It really hurt when she said this, and I think I panicked a bit. You know, she was right when I looked in the mirror later in the evening; there was a lot more of me to hold on to, so I started swimming more and drinking less. I lost a stone and bought some new clothes, but I still didn't feel like I used to. I kept thinking about what Julie said, 'We're not kids any longer', and that started me worrying about things I never thought about before: what happens when the kids grow up, what if I get sick and can't work, do I really like what I'm doing or does it just put food on the table, what if I stop fancying Julie?

One of my friends at work was having an affair with one of the sales staff, and he would cry on my shoulder about his problems. I began to think that maybe that was what I needed, especially after I lost all the weight, but the truth was I didn't really want to. There was a woman on my route who was obviously interested and I thought about it quite seriously, and this is the strangest thing of all. I talked it over with my parish priest! It's not the kind of thing that guys I know do, talk to a minister about sex, but we've known him for a long time. He baptized the kids and I go to church a few times a month to keep my hand in; I don't approve of these families who just send their kids along to Sunday School and then pick them up at the door after it's over. He's in his fifties I guess, married and divorced, so I figured he wouldn't be too shocked about what I was feeling. I was knocked back when he said yes, I could do that and it might be nice, but maybe there were bigger issues around for me. Well, that just opened it all up for me because that's exactly what I was feeling, so after talking with him a few times I got up the courage to talk to Julie about where our lives together were going.

Lately I've been feeling a lot better. Julie told me things about myself and about us that I never thought I'd hear her say. She was bored, not with me, but with what she was getting out of life. Not that she was unhappy with the life we had built together, but that she was feeling that there must be more for her than managing the kids, running the house, and choosing new carpet. We didn't need the money, but she thought she might go back to work which meant that someone would have to take care of the kids more often. Then I thought, 'I'd like to do that; I hardly know what their lives are like'. The strange thing was that I was really excited about the changes we were talking about; they weren't things I ever thought I would want to do, but it was exciting to know that we could change our lives if we wanted to. So now I look in the mirror and I see this thirty-six-year-old guy whose hair is almost gone, who gets bone tired at the end of the day at work and with the kids, and whose face is beginning to look like a road map of wrinkles, and I think, 'You're doing alright Murray; you're not a kid anymore . . . thank God for that'.

Murray's road through his mid-life negotiation is common to many men's experiences but has unique elements. It must be said that he brought a good deal of insight into the process from the beginning, but he was also courageous enough to be able to stand back and to observe the process while experiencing it. Looking for someone outside his daily routine with whom to discuss his feelings was a key element in the successful reordering of his life. It did not have to be his parish priest, but Murray was wise to look for someone who was caring but not involved or judgemental about the outcome of his process. The other key element of Murray's reaction to his mid-life change was his ability to talk with his partner about his feelings without fear; this opened up an area for discussion previously avoided by the couple. The choice on his part was to give his wife the opportunity to be frank about where she found herself as part of a couple and as an individual. The outcomes for Murray are those which many men in mid-life attest to: a lessening of tension in their relationship, a renewed sense of vigour, a change of focus from outside concerns to the concerns about the inner life of human beings as shown in his deeper involvement with his children, and a sense of power and control over their lives in a way they had not experienced previously. And all this began because Murray was worrying about getting fat.

Likewise, physical changes can trigger mid-life changes for women. There are definite physiological changes for women during and after childbearing, and these influence the mid-life process as well. Women are the largest group of people *diagnosed* with depression in this country and are often treated with a variety of drugs. In our opinion, this is not always helpful because the medication can mask the call to making a mid-life renegotiation. Our bodies may well be sending us a message which we respond to by loading it with chemicals rather than looking at other aspects of our lives. There is far too much tinkering with the hormonal balance of women and far too little listening to the inner voice which begins to make itself known in mid-life. On the other hand, many women report a new sense of confidence and power as they enter their mid-years. When a woman can look at her first stage of life and value her accomplishments – career, children, relationships – then she is able to move more comfortably into the first stage of mid-life renegotiation. One of the most positive elements of most women's lives are their interconnecting relationships with families and other women, an area where men report a sense of emptiness and lack of fulfilment. Building on these relationships, a woman can begin to consider options for the second stage of her life. If there are children and/or a permanent relationship, these are usually stabilized by the early thirties, and it is time for women to make decisions about where their journeys might lead them next.

The advent of a major illness for a man or woman can be the catalyst for growth especially if it comes near the end of the first stage of life. Such an event can be looked on as creative illness and it may be the beginning point for a deep examination of life. One of the unique qualities about a hospital stay is that we are rendered powerless. Our clothes are taken away, meal times and menus are dictated for us, and the programme of care is decided by the medical staff. This is very difficult for most people as these are areas we usually control and they give us a sense of power over the circumstances of life. One of the ways in which a major illness can be used is as a time to step back and to reflect on what has gone before and what will come. Half of the work is already done for us as we have been pulled out of daily routine by the illness. At this time it is almost impossible not to drop one's defences and to muse about life. There is also the fact that there is little else to do in an NHS hospital bed or when one is confined to bed at home. Frequently these events catch us off guard and we are propelled into mid-life without ever realizing what is happening. There is a school of thought which holds that we can literally give ourselves illness, and it is important to look at the role a mid-life illness is playing in our lives. The psychological term for this is somatizing, and it is important to understand that such illnesses are quite real and can represent displaced feelings from our inner lives. This means quite simply that feelings can produce anxiety or they can be re-routed through the body to produce illness. Whether or not this is true, it is helpful to look at your illness and to ask some important questions and to see if your inner voice gives any answers: 'Why am I ill at this particular time?', 'What else is going on in life that I find difficult to manage?', 'Why this type of illness?', 'Am I asking for help in some other area and using the illness as a means of getting it?' Sometimes this can be done alone, but more often it is best to look to someone who can explore these questions dispassionately and make suggestions or observations from outside the situation. The important element in major illness in mid-life is not to be afraid of it and to see it as the beginning of the new. Major illness may well contain the seeds of new growth, and at the very least the time spent examining the questions suggested above will give a clearer picture as to what issues might be around.

Susan's story is complex but one that demonstrates how a combination of single events can work together to facilitate a positive mid-life change. She married Lawrence in her early twenties and quickly had two children, both boys. Her husband had a career in the military and they travelled extensively for fifteen years until he was mustered out a few years ago during one of the Government cutbacks in the military budget. Theirs had always been a loving and caring relationship, and she describes herself as quite happy. They moved to Scotland while Lawrence looked for work and it was at this time that Susan's father died. She had not been close to her father, quite the opposite as he was an alcoholic and very distant from his children. Susan had early on become the 'little mother' of the family and felt that she was never 'special' because she was too busy taking care of her three siblings, a dependent mother and a volatile, unstable father. She escaped this environment when she married Lawrence, but not surprisingly she took on the same role in her own family. She calls herself 'Supermum'. 'I never complained about all the moving we had to do in our marriage; it was just part of our lives and actually I found it quite exciting sometimes. The only thing that bothered me was that the boys kept changing schools and friends, and I was determined that they would have a happy childhood, unlike my own.' What a happy childhood meant for Susan was a life characterized by physical affection, listening parents who were interested in the boys' lives, and clear, fair and consistent boundaries and rules. She and Lawrence were able to provide this for their sons, and she says she feels confident that they have given them the best upbringing they could have. Obviously Susan feels that their family life has been a shared effort and that she has accomplished a good deal in the first stage of her life.

Perhaps this was the reason she was so dismayed at the level of grief and abandonment she felt when her father died. Eighteen months later she was still feeling that her life had lost meaning and she was quite angry. Angry because she had never loved her father and she felt it wasn't fair that she should be so controlled by her feelings of unreasonable grief for the father she never had. Her father's death occurred at the same time as Lawrence's redundancy which added even more pressure to the situation; Susan also felt since her grief was unjustified that she couldn't share it with anyone. The third element which triggered Susan's re-examination was a series of physical problems which started with urinary infections and proceeded to endometriosis and finally to her consultant advising a hysterectomy at the age of forty. Susan is fortunate in that she and Lawrence do talk about their lives, and he sensed that things were not right for her. He suggested that she might like to consider doing the degree course she had always dreamed of since they had his mustering out settlement, and she entered a local university to do a degree in sociology with a view to teaching.

For a time this seemed to solve many of the problems Susan was experiencing; she was so busy with her university work that she pushed her grief, sadness and worry about her physical problems to the bottom of her personal agenda. However, this did not last for long. She was very successful in her course work, enjoyed meeting younger students, and the challenges of the intellectual life; however, she was still plagued by periods of sadness. 'It was not depression and I didn't tell my doctor about it because he would try to fill me up with pills. I knew I needed something, but I was sure I didn't need to hide behind tranquillizers or painkillers. I've seen too many of my friends go down that road to be fooled into thinking it would help me.' What Susan was experiencing was what we would call 'an accumulation of sadness'. The death of her father put her in touch with feelings of early deprivation and inappropriate responsibility as a young girl which she had kept bottled up for years. She had attempted subconsciously to expiate these feelings by giving her sons a loving and caring parental home, and in some degree this did help rid her of a little of the anger about her own childhood. However, we cannot emphasize enough the power of the experience of early childhood deprivation and its lasting effects.

One day in her second year of university Susan found herself sitting in a lecture when she was overcome with her feelings of sadness; she began to cry, gently at first, and then quite openly. She had to leave and retreated to the loo where she spent the next few hours hiding her tears and anger behind a closed door. 'I thought to myself, "This can't go on; I'm ruining my life; I have to get a hold of myself", so I did something I thought I would never do. I went to the student counselling service and someone saw me right away. I sat in her office for an hour and just cried. I felt such a pillock!' For Susan this was the beginning of her mid-life change; a change that is interesting because it is about changing

54

her inner world rather than her outer one. She already had done much good work on the outside with her family, her degree course and the relationship with Lawrence, but she had closed off the inner voice which was calling her to renegotiate what had gone before in the first stage of life. What began for Susan was a series of counselling sessions where she could share what she was feeling without fear of judgement; as she grew in confidence and respect for her feelings she joined a therapy group at the university where her maturity and courage were valued by other group members. In the group she was able to speak about always being 'the good little girl' and to try out some new behaviour where she allowed herself to feel special and to be irresponsible. At the same time her counsellor suggested she might want to talk to the university chaplain about her feelings of grief and that has proved a fruitful relationship. Susan had been raised in a strict religious regime and the disparity between the love talked about in Scripture and the reality of her life in the congregation had made her cynical and angry towards the Church. She still saw herself as a Christian but had not attended church in years. 'The chaplain was a great woman really; I didn't know women could be chaplains, but she sorted me out soon enough. She just took me where I was and didn't try to fit me into some convenient pattern of grief therapy. I guess I just rambled on about what a nasty person God must be. Anyway, I still see her from time to time and it feels good that she knows how I'm doing. There was no magic cure, but it was useful.' One of the most useful roles a clergy-person can play is that of being the container for strong and often negative feelings about God and the Church. Susan found someone who could accept without defending their corner, and through that acceptance she came to understand more clearly the loving God we as Christians know.

One of the most important realizations which physical changes and losses bring to us is that we are half-way into life. This is often a difficult thing to accept as most of us do not dwell on the finite quality of life. However, life does end and is quite brief, but that is one of the qualities about life which enhances its beauty and gives it meaning. The reaction to this realization can be panic and a sense of time fleeting away, and all this is quite true; however,

55

there is a more creative response. This is to say to oneself, 'Yes, I'm half-way there, but half-way to where?' From one point of view we are half-way to death and the loss of all the love and beauty of what we know as life. It is easy to dwell on this existential certainty and many people find themselves caught in what philosophers and theologians call 'existential *angst*'. What this means quite simply is that we can feel the beauty and wonder of life so deeply that when faced with the prospect of its ending we are made impotent with terror and pain. The nature of human consciousness is that we are given the opportunity to choose personal values with which to face an apparently absurd world and we are tormented by feelings of anguish and disgust. The authors have seen innumerable people for counselling and care who are frozen in this state and their lives are damaged and diminished by this sense of fragility. Mothers look at their children and realize that they may well not live to see their grandchildren full grown. Family gatherings which include several generations can be affirming and positive events, but they can also bring the pain of the knowledge that people grow old, change and die – that life never remains the same.

Our family which opened this chapter shares the pictures of the parents' adolescence and the laughter of the adults is tinged with a deep sense of loss and fear about what is to come so quickly. This is all quite natural and all a part of the journey of life, but when dealt with creatively it can lead to a renewed sense of one's own personal power and worth. The German-American theologian Paul Tillich wrote a small book concerning this issue called *The Courage To Be*. Although couched in theological language it says simply that at some point we must do the courageous thing, which is accepting and living with knowledge of death and loss, rather than denying it or running away from it. When we have done this, then we can begin to live. Perhaps the mid-life men and women who spend money on anti-ageing beauty products, those who spend hours at the fitness centre exercising away excess poundage, and those who adopt dress styles much too young for their age would be better off using the same energy to tackle courageously the business of negotiating the second stage of life.

The prize to be gained at the end of this challenge is the confidence of middle age. This sense of confidence is highly underrated and it is good to listen to someone who has struggled and who values the second stage of life highly.

My name is Christopher and I'm forty-eight. I don't want this to sound like a confession or a religious witness story, but I want to tell other men and women what it was like for me. When I was forty-two I was three stone heavier, I smoked a fair amount, I was successful in my career, I had, still had, a good marriage and two lovely daughters . . . and I was frightened all the time. I was frightened that someone would find out that I was a fraud. That I wasn't the successful, strong, God-fearing, suburban business-man that I appeared to be. That just below the thin surface of my life was the class sissy, the pimply faced boy whom everyone kicked around the school yard, the adolescent who masturbated every night after his mother ordered him off to bed, the university graduate who barely got a pass degree. When I left school I decided that I was tired of being a loser all my life, so I looked around to see what made people popular and successful. What I came up with was an agenda set by my family, society, and the Church which encouraged the maintenance of a consistent façade of competence and confidence; you had to keep a lot of balls in the air at the same time but it was possible. So, I went at it and it worked, but the price was high. I always felt like someone was breathing down my neck ready to expose me for the liar and fraud that I was hiding. Once or twice I went out with mates and got very drunk and some of them said the same thing, but then the next day we would pretend it didn't happen. And soon we drifted apart. It seemed that when we came close to sharing our real feelings and insecurities the danger became too great and we had to flee one another. It's quite lonely out there for most men, I think. I'd heard about the Men's Movement in the States and part of me was quite attracted, but I couldn't imagine myself dressing up like a Red Indian and beating a drum in the forest. But there was something about what they were saying that spoke to part of me, that part that I kept hidden. However, I was working so hard keeping the juggling balls in the air that there wasn't any room for self-indulgent navel gazing.

Then the most amazing thing happened. One night, about three in the morning, I had a telephone call which brought me quickly out of my usual three-gin-and-tonic-induced sleep. It was from an old university mate, Bob, who I had known from schooldays. He was my only friend from the past as he had been the kid they bullied in the form just above me. We had ended up at the same university where he transformed himself into one of the most handsome and successful undergraduates in our college, but by then he didn't want to know me. Well, at first I thought he was drunk, but it soon became clear that he was crying. The story tumbled out that he had been having problems with a rebellious daughter; she was out on school nights drinking and having sex with her friends. She had come in that evening after midnight with her underclothes in her hand, and Bob had hit her. She hit him back and went to her room. Since then he had been walking around central London wondering what he was going to do, how he had done such a thing, where had it all gone wrong. Then he thought of me and rang. I listened to him talk about how hard he had to work to hold his life together, how afraid he was to talk to anyone about his fears, and he finally confessed that the reason he rang me was because I was the only person he thought was a bigger loser than him. I had to laugh at that, and so did he. We agreed to meet after work the following night, but I didn't really expect him to show. I'd had my experiences with men letting down their defences before, and I knew what would happen, but I went to the pub anyway.

Bob did show and we began meeting each week for a moan. At first it was very tentative and it took a lot of courage to say some of the things that we needed to get off our chests. We finally decided that a pub wasn't the best place for this kind of talking, so we started jogging together at Crystal Palace on Sunday mornings. Sometimes it was very heavy emotionally and other times it was just moaning about our families, work and what a drag it was being over forty. Then we got into what our dreams had been and how we had accomplished a lot of them, but without any sense of fulfilment. From there it went to fantasies about what we'd really like from life and it came out that we just wanted to be loved for what we were, not what we could do or produce. Changes started happening slowly, and I mark it as the time we finally began to trust one another. The big issues for us were the past, how much we had hated and still hated our childhoods. We both shared a sense that somehow we had deserved the bullying we got at school and that we never had an opportunity to find out who we really were. As we began to do this our wives noticed a change in our attitude to work and at home. Both of us began to want to spend more time with other people rather than concentrating on work or jobs around the house. My wife said one evening after we had lingered at the dinner table for a hour, 'You know Chris, I think you've found a sense of humour; I didn't think it was possible. Maybe you should go jogging with Bob twice a week'. As Bob began to listen to what was inside him, he was able to hear what his daughter was saying and their relationship improved. One of the good things is that we both lost weight and stopped smoking, and now we look like prime middle-age specimens of *Suburbanitcus Britannica*.

What do I think happened to us? Well, I think that by sharing the fears that we were carrying around inside for so long, it released them somehow. As I realized I wasn't alone and wasn't a freak, I came to accept that I had accomplished a lot despite the pain of my past. That pain hasn't been removed, I don't think it ever could be, but I am able to accept that it is part of me and part of what makes me a strong man. I also realized that I quite like being a man and being around other men, especially men who aren't afraid to show their feelings. For a while it worried me that Bob and I had become so close, and what other people might say about us. We talked about sex a lot after we got to trust one another and we said a lot which will always remain private, but I will tell you that neither of us feel we are sexually attracted to men. However, I can say comfortably that I love Bob, so if you want to call that 'gay' that's your problem. Slowly I began to relax into a new confidence about myself, and a new confidence about my capacity to change and to grow. I began to look for new challenges, ones that I could share with my wife and daughters.

59

We started doing summer home exchanges with families around the world, and next year we are exchanging homes, jobs and lifestyles with a family in upstate New York for the entire year. We are all looking forward to it. I can't say how important the friendship with Bob has been.

The confidence which Bob and Christopher feel has been created out of a unique healing relationship which took a good deal of courage on both men's part. Rather than being lucky, they were courageous enough to reach out to find a companion for their mid-life renegotiation. This type of bonding can and does happen between women more commonly, but it can take many forms. Not everyone will need to join a support group, seek counselling, or spiritual direction – or even read this book. However, for many people there needs to be a catalyst for change. In Bob's case it was losing control with his daughter, for Susan it was the death of her father, and for Julie and Murray it was changes in physical appearance and stamina. All these men and women have been able to come to terms with their first stage of life without throwing away the benefits and accomplishments they have achieved. As they move well into middle age it is with an enviable sense of confidence about the future and the possibilities it will bring. Their sense of time slipping away and of wasting the best years of their lives has lessened. In Tillich's frame of reference they have accepted the courage to be.

4

SPIRITUALITY

Our relationship with God is one which is characterized by change and growth as we grow in our understanding and experience. The God we knew in our childhood is most certainly not the God we would recognize as adults. Likewise for many the model held of God begins to change in mid-life as we change and age. This is not to say that God changes, but rather our relationship with God is in constant revision as we go through life. This can be an unsettling concept for some as they have a need to hang on to a sense of security in a complex and confusing world. However, it must be understood that as we continue to interact with Scripture, the tradition of the Church and our own experience through prayer, study and meditation we begin to know God in different ways.

If this is true, and the authors assert that in our experience and in the lives of those with whom we have worked it is, the question must be asked, is there a spirituality of mid-life and, if so, what does it look like? This chapter will discuss this question, drawing on the experiences of men and women who have maintained and renewed a faith in God as they encounter mid-life renegotiation.

There seem to be two common experiences at this point in life: either one deepens one's faith or one loses faith. The loss of faith and religious expression of that faith is quite common to middle-aged people. Among one of the most common reasons is that the ties that bind them to Church and God may have been held loosely in the first place. Attendance at church may have been a matter of social convention, doing what's expected of families in the area: children may be grown now and off on their own and the impetus to attend regularly for their sake or for their activities no longer exists. Slowly the habit is broken until the only times church is on the agenda is Easter and Christmas as well as the occasional wedding, funeral or baptism. There seems to be little to hold and to interest people in many churches today, especially if their commitment was a casual one to begin with.

Very often as people enter middle age, they experience their first death, usually a parent or friend. The shock of these losses can be so overwhelming that if the solace offered by the Church does not meet a person's need he or she will feel shortchanged by God. Anger and guilt result, and sometimes the relationship is permanently severed. In this situation so much depends on the type of pastoring offered to people at vulnerable times. It is difficult for the minister to know whether he or she is offering too much, being too intrusive, or is being seen as distant and unhelpful. There is much sentimental rephrasing of Scriptural assurances of God's continuing love and care for us, but when faced with the emptiness of losing someone who is central to our lives, it is difficult for many people to see that this is true. They most likely are looking for God to act as a divine interventionist to take away the pain and sense of loss, and the question must be asked whether they have not been led to believe that this would happen. False assurances of life lived without pain are of little help when faced with the reality of life: the death of a child, parents, or a close friend. The inability of the Church adequately to explain the problem of evil and pain in the world in words which most people can understand also leads to this feeling of being abandoned by God. One of the authors once made the comment at a church gathering that he was plagued by a fear of flying which was a real problem since he flew so much. A pious lady overheard and was indignant that a priest could be so concerned about death. She assured him that Jesus was waiting just outside the window of the plane to accept him into heaven if the 747 should crash. This silly example of even sillier, childish faith statements which carry even less import than their words mean, does bring up an important problem: if as Christians we look forward to a life beyond this one lived in the knowledge and love of God, what is there to worry about in this world? The authors would answer this with two clichés just as silly and just as important: we don't believe in a 'Pie in the Sky' God; we believe in a 'Jam Today, Jam Tomorrow' God. We don't live in a world filled with pain and sorrow so we will be rewarded in the next life; we live in a world of beauty and joy, wonder and creative energy, as well as one filled with contradiction, loss and pain. Our lives are just the beginning of a long progression, or pilgrimage if you will, to joining God. And that is why it does not show a lack of faith to be scared out of your wits when you are encased in a small metal tube 30,000 feet above the earth's surface going along at 800 kilometres an hour.

A person's faith can be deepened in mid-life for many of the same reasons discussed above. The first encounter with death can bring people to consider the important questions surrounding the meaning of life. Few of us focus on death until it enters our life in a concrete way, but once the challenge is presented it can lead to a renewed understanding of one's faith. As discussed in previous chapters, mid-life is often about questioning the assumptions and priorities made in the first stage of life, and for many people their adult spirituality is formed during this time. It is often a spirituality of abundance, of celebration of the opportunities in life. When the focus is on building permanent relationships, the birth of children and working hard to achieve career goals, it is easy to see life as one long, logical progression towards some restful and peaceful state of plenty. In mid-life these assumptions are often shattered by death, failure, or an experience of the ageing process. What seemed possible and desirable in the first stage of life holds questionable value in the afternoon. The call here is to develop a deeper understanding of Scripture and to relate it to the experience of life.

David and Gwenth started appearing in church after Easter; they must have been around before but no one had noticed them until they started coming regularly to the Sunday morning eight o'clock service and again for the Wednesday evening Eucharist. They were a mystery to the rest of the congregation and all attempts to get them involved in church activities failed. Everyone was surprised when they volunteered to join the church's pledged giving scheme the following year. However, to the credit of their fellow parishioners they were not pressed about church outings, theatre parties and parish suppers, but left on their own to come and go as they wished. Everyone assumed they were married, but they made an odd couple. Both were in their late thirties or early forties, Gwenth was short and square with a very practical approach to dressing, plain sensible outfits in brown or grey. By contrast David was a fashion plate, tall and thin with long elegant hands. He often wore flamboyant scarfs and a beautiful belted cashmere overcoat which hid what seemed to be richly patterned shirts. However, his most outstanding feature was his shoulder-length grey hair which he alternately wore loose or pulled back in a trendy pony tail. Not your usual church-going couple to say the least. They kept to themselves, paid their pledges, and occasionally would attend a church event.

Eventually they came to the curate to discuss questions which they had about some of the theology in the Eucharistic prayer, and their stories unfolded. Both were in the throes of mid-life renegotiation and a reclaiming of their faith seemed to be quite central to their experience. As it turned out they were not married, or even lovers, 'just old friends' Gwenth said, but friends who were sharing the fellowship of a journey into mid-life. Gwenth was a teacher who had just finished training as a psychotherapist and was in the process of setting up a private practice. She was single and lived all her life with a mother who had given birth to Gwenth well after she was forty. 'I guess I'll always be single; marriage was never even presented as an option to me; someone had to take care of Mum. I went to teachers' college so I could support us both, and it hasn't been a bad life. I loved my Mum and she wasn't difficult to take care of, at least not until the last year before she died.' When Gwenth adjusted to living alone she began to think about the rest of her life; now that she was alone she could do as she liked, and she began the process of renegotiating her life for the second stage. An interest in counselling led her to train as a psychotherapist, and her mother's death brought her into contact with the Church. The contact developed into questioning and finally studying and attending the Eucharist to see where it would lead.

David and Gwenth had met at teacher training college but his life had been very different. His first teaching job was in the

Middle East, followed by Africa, Australasia and Canada. At forty he had not formed any significant relationships although he said he had a series of 'liaisons' over the years, but they never lead to anything permanent. During his travels he had become a Buddhist and had considered becoming a monk at one point. A year ago his current teaching contract had ended, and he found himself at forty living in a foreign country without any roots and without any real direction to his life. David returned to the UK where he renewed his friendship with Gwenth and was currently renting a room in her house while he was doing supply teaching. What had seemed like a glamorous life without commitments and filled with new experiences, travel and excitement of new friends and work each year had left him with a feeling of emptiness and loneliness. He felt that his attraction to Buddhism reflected his former life goals, and he was searching for a more direct relationship with a God who is active in this world. It was the ageing process which brought David to his mid-life renegotiation rather than any dramatic event.

These two people, then, were looking to enrich their lives in the second stage through examination and exploration of the past. David wanted to reclaim his Christian roots and Gwenth was interested to see where being a Christian would fit into her new life as a therapist. Single people often feel the mid-life process in a very deep way as they are less connected through a permanent relationship. David and Gwenth were eager to make changes in their lives and to make use of the Christian tradition for that purpose. They were looking for a mid-life spirituality which spoke to them as single people, not one which only affirmed family life and community responsibility. Many people come to mid-life seeking a personal and individual relationship with God. It is not surprising that David was drawn to the mystical and transcendental aspects of Christianity while Gwenth was looking at the teaching and healing ministry of Jesus. Neither was interested in moral theology drawn from Scripture although they did appreciate its place in the tradition. Both were looking to see where they might fit in life and in the Church.

If you look at the typical congregation in this country, you will see mainly the faces of women. In the suburbs there are clusters of family-centred congregations, but even there the women will always outnumber the men. This is ironic because the Church hierarchy is male dominated as is much of the theology, and this won't change very quickly even with the ordination of women in the past year. So the situation is that we have a male-dominated institution which ministers to congregations largely made up of women. Obviously, the disparity points out that men either don't feel comfortable in the Church or the Church has little to offer them. There is a growing concern about this issue, and a good deal of it comes from men themselves, both inside and outside the Church. The Church talks about feelings and God in a way which men often find difficult to accept. Most men live in a very competitive world in the first stage of their lives: there is competition to succeed in education, on the sports ground, in the search for a partner and, of course, in the work place. Very little credit is given to the spirit of co-operation, and men find themselves caught in the void between what they feel inside and what the world expects of them. The language of the Church is often one which stresses feelings and working together, but at the same time success is valued highly. Successful businessmen are usually expected to take leadership roles in their congregations, and they are often asked to lead membership or fund drives which call on their skills in winning. Their church lives become an extension of their secular lives, rather than a place to test and explore their sensitivity and emotional side of their nature.

Men are encouraged on the one hand to enter the inner world where emotions and sensation reign but on the other the skills they are asked by the Church to exercise are in just the opposite areas. Church life for men should present new territory to explore rather than repeating the old emotional ground they know already. There are also very few opportunities for men to share together in a non-threatening context with other men. If men do become involved in church groups and want to exercise their 'feeling side' the model offered to them is a feminine one, and they are allowed to become honorary women for a short period of time. Opportunities for men to develop their own models of expression and to share with one another need to be provided as men do have something to say about their faith. Men of faith often have half a lifetime of suppressed feelings about God, their lives and their faith to express and they are given little opportunity to do so. The advent of mid-life is a time when it seems particularly appropriate for these areas to be explored, and it is our sense and experience that men are just waiting for the chance. Stephen's story is one which demonstrates the hidden and unexpressed depths which lie just beneath the surface of many men experiencing a mid-life renegotiation.

As the reader approached the lectern, I thought to myself that if I have to sit through the story of the prodigal son one more time I shall get up and scream. I didn't scream but I did get up and walk out. Right down the centre aisle of the church, out into the graveyard, and back to my house and garden. My wife and children must have thought I'd flipped, and when they came home I couldn't talk about it. I just said I needed some fresh air, but my wife knows my family history and she must have understood. She's heard the stories over and over, and it never does any good; the anger and frustration are still with me and she just feels worse because she can't help.

I grew up in a family that had a prodigal son . . . and it wasn't me. I was the good one; the one who did not squander his inheritance, the one who was always there when the family needed me, the successful one at school, the one who made a good marriage and established a life in the town where I grew up. I always remember competing with my brother for my parents' affection; don't get me wrong, they loved me. But my brother could cock up everything, get drunk, steal, disappear for weeks, and he would always get the extra attention that I craved. It never seemed fair that he should be so irresponsible, and, as I saw it then, reap the reward of my parents' non-judgemental love. So when the Old Testament lesson came round each year to the prodigal son I would seethe with rage and anger, and that morning I just couldn't take it any more. Perhaps because it was my fortieth birthday as well, but I thought to myself that even on my bloody birthday I am robbed of feeling special by my prodigal brother.

The other tension inside of me then was also triggered by a Scriptural story, the relationship between Jonathan and David.

Each time I would encounter that passage I would experience a deep sense of loneliness inside and a longing for a brother or friendship like they shared. I know some people interpret that story to mean that they had a physical relationship and that may be, but that isn't what attracted me. I read into their friendship a possibility for sharing and support that I had never experienced with other men, and neither had any of my friends. The idea of opening up to another man, even a fellow Christian, made me feel much too vulnerable and weak, so I just kept it all bottled up inside. That is I did until I turned forty when I began to look at my life and to get in touch with my feelings of being cheated by life. Why is it that men always have to be in charge and take the responsibility? I was sick and tired of being the one who had to make the decisions about where we would live, whether it was going to be a foreign holiday or not, if the children were going to private school, even whether or not my wife and I would have sex of an evening. And my marriage was one of the better ones as far as I could see, but the assumption was that I would propose a course of action, then we would discuss it, and a decision would be made together . . . but I felt, at forty, the weight of years of leading our family through life.

The Church wasn't any help, although it was one of the few places where I could be alone and inside myself for an hour or so; however, there is a strong unstated assumption that Christian men are to be proactive in the way that Scripture is interpreted. It seemed to be a conspiracy to keep me in the role of the good son throughout my life; where was the freedom that is talked about so much in the New Testament? I was even envious of Jesus which is very strange for someone whose faith has always played a central role. The way he is depicted as moving into people's lives and coming alongside them without threatening or intimidating them, this was what I wanted. I wanted to be with men and women as an equal, living in an atmosphere of empowerment and co-operation . . . it all sounds very 'mid-life crisis', doesn't it? I was caught somewhere between what I was and what I wanted to be with absolutely no clear view of how to move forward. Prayer was no help because my prayer life had dried up years ago, pastoral counselling seemed like a joke and, besides, our parish priest was far too busy ministering to crisis after crisis in the parish. My male friends would listen once, then I was sure they'd retreat into their own isolated worlds, and that left my wife.

After my birthday supper, my wife and I went off to bed, but I just lied there staring at the ceiling. Then out of the blue she said, 'It's your brother Frank, isn't it?' I crossed my arms over my chest and grunted agreement. She got up and closed our bedroom door. 'I know Frank isn't here; I know no one knows where he's been for the past five years, but why don't you tell him what you're feeling tonight. I'll be Frank.' I sat on the edge of the bed and looked at her and I could see Frank's face instead of hers, his handsome feckless expression admitting that he'd messed up again and wanted to be forgiven. The dammed feelings inside burst out and thirty minutes later I was still at it until I was covered in sweat and exhausted. What happened next I'm not going to talk about, but for once in my life I didn't have to be in charge.

The next morning I felt more free and released that I had in years, and I wanted to find some way to keep that feeling with me. My wife said she had an idea and to leave it to her. The week went well and next Sunday in church I sat in the pew reading the weekly notices and saw an announcement: *Sharing our stories: Men interested in forming a confidential, leaderless group to share their personal journeys in life are invited to meet Wednesday evening at 74 East End Lane, 7.00 pm.* It took me a few seconds to realize that it was our address in the announcement, and my wife just sat there looking quite pleased with herself. I thought this is the best birthday gift I've had in years; I would never have summoned the courage to do it myself, and I know I would have felt responsible for the success of the group if I had.

Five men showed up the first evening. It took some time to decide what the group rules might be, and it took even longer for us to begin to trust one another to say what we were feeling. Now, three years down the road, there are seven of us who meet regularly at different houses for a couple of hours every fortnight. There is nothing forbidden as topics of conversation and everyone gets an opportunity to use some time if they need it. Mainly it's about moving into middle age as an average Christian man, which means the issues are the same as they would be for any man: power versus co-operation, sexuality, fear of ageing, past pain and loss, how our faith fits into our lives, what we want to do with the second part of our lives. It is good and it's good that it's remained a small group. Last month, our vicar took me aside and asked if he could come along if he didn't wear his collar!

The role played by Stephen's wife in the above story introduces the changing role of women in our society and in the Church from servant/helper to leader/facilitator, which represents a healthy movement in our society. It can be seen as a trickle down effect of the women's movement since the Second World War. A generation of women was expected to return to house and hearth in the 1950s, but many found that while there is fulfilment in traditional roles there are other options open for them. Their daughters are now well into middle age, and their granddaughters have had the benefit of two generations who have chipped away at the traditional roles expected of women. While men need to learn and to experience more in the areas of sharing and serving, women are feeling the need to lead and to be active participants in their own faith journeys, rather than being passive assistants. One clear example of this trend is the growth in the number of women presenting themselves for training for full-time ministry. The first women were ordained as priests in the Church of England last year, and this heralds what is hoped to be a significant challenge to the male-dominated hierarchy. In other denominations and in other branches of the Anglican Communion, Christians have had the benefit of the full ministry of women for over twenty years. There are even women bishops in North America and New Zealand. Stephen's wife is probably more typical of Christian women today in that she is able to choose when to lead and when to follow, an option not always open in the past. Once women are able to move past the anger of years of living with a spiritual agenda set by men, they are able to work creatively in their own lives and in the lives of others. What they bring to this new role is a deep understanding of being marginal, of the joys of serving and facilitating, and an identification with the lonely, the powerless and those who find solidarity in their shared lives. Women have been a major force in the growth of Christian counselling, spiritual direction, and social justice issues, but they are now moving into traditionally male-dominated areas as well.

While it would be easy to choose a glamorous figure to illustrate these changes, such as one of the women bishops overseas or one of the older women who broke the barriers in the 1960s, we feel it is more helpful and more realistic to hear the story of Joy, a lively and attractive woman in her thirties who was ordained as an Anglican priest last year after waiting as a deacon since she left training college in 1988. Joy offered herself for training in her late twenties after a career in teaching. She had been raised in a Christian family within the evangelical tradition; the only unusual aspect of her upbringing was that her father was a popular vicar in South London. The choice of a teaching career in primary school is a common option for women as it is one of the acceptable areas in which women are allowed to excel, most likely because the job focuses on caring for children, and until just recently it has been an area which men did not enter. Fortunately, this is changing also. The decision to train for ministry was not an easy one for Joy as she was raised within a tradition which relegated women to assisting and enabling roles, and many evangelicals still have problems allowing women to exercise leadership. Her time at theological college marks a significant period of growth for her as she came into contact with a wide variety of spiritual traditions.

> At that time Cranmer Hall in Durham was quite open and it was a breath of fresh air to meet men and women from Catholic, low church, the Church of Wales, and the States; this made me examine my own roots and to sort out what was good about them and what no longer fit for me. It was at this time that my spirituality began to change as I was exposed to expressions of faith quite different from my own. There were several men from the Catholic wing of the C of E and I found them personally charming, good fun, and with some very interesting theological ideas. I had never thought about the sacraments in quite the way they did, and it was creative to hear them explain incarnation and sacramental

theology as it was lived out in their lives. It was also a threatening time because it gave me the freedom to look at what I really believed – that is one of the really good things about theological college. From time to time, I would retreat back into the safe evangelical world of my childhood and early life, and I will always value my roots . . . but I have grown and changed. Much of this growth and change is directly related to my experience as a woman and specifically as a Christian woman.

For Joy, as for many women, as she entered her early thirties she began to examine what had gone before and to think about the next stage of life. However, for most of us this is a gradual process; not one where we wake up one morning, deciding to leave one career and begin another, or perhaps we encounter disparity between our experience and our faith beliefs, then set about logically making changes. One of the gifts of age is both the heightened sense of time, and the knowledge that process is as important as the changes which it produces. Joy's journey has taken almost ten years, but she is quite a different person now from when she began. In addition, Joy would say that she never envisioned the results of her mid-life renegotiation to look quite like they do, but she is pleased with where she has arrived. We can begin with one agenda and one set of goals and they can change dramatically as we move along.

I never thought I would get to the point where I could no longer call myself an evangelical; that particular label had been such an important part of my upbringing and my identity. As I grew in confidence to listen to what my inner life was telling me, I found that I was no longer comfortable putting myself inside of a safe boxed set of beliefs. While at training college I began to accept leadership roles which was not necessarily new for me, but the committee work on a national level brought me in contact with lots of different people. While at college I worked with a group of representatives from all the theological colleges; I became associated with the women's ordination movement and I now serve on the General Synod. My growth has not been without its sadness and losses; some of my friends do not share my views about women's leadership roles, and my determination to remain in touch with my own inner direction has made it difficult to establish a permanent relationship. Who wants to marry a woman vicar? And if they do, are they the kind of man I would want to marry?

Joy's Christmas letter to her friends was a good indication of the success of her mid-life change; it reveals a woman who is quite clear about her current priorities, who enjoys life and skiing holidays with friends, and one who keeps in touch with her family and spiritual roots while living to a new agenda. Currently Joy describes the important issues for her to be in the areas of the role of women in the Church, working with other Christians to move along the discussion of sexuality, and her continuing commitment to social justice issues. After five years of work as a deacon in an inner-city community centre which included a ministry to drug users and single-parent families, she has moved to a more traditional parish in South London to exercise her priestly ministry. While not all women want to be ordained ministers, Joy's story highlights the options open for change in women's spiritual lives. Mid-life can be the most exciting period for many women as they bring emotional and experiential resources to the process which are unique to their lives as women; one of the gifts women have to bring from their spiritual lives are these resources and men can benefit from taking advantage of them.

This chapter's focus is spirituality rather than religious practice, and it is true that most people in our society, while admitting to believing in God or to possessing some type of personal, private spirituality, do not attend Church. There are many others who deny the use and importance of the transcendent in their lives. This will be a most difficult discussion for the authors because we have always had a living relationship with God which is worked out through participation in regular worship. However, we realize this is not the case for most people. When talking with men and women as they move into mid-life it is a common scenario for them to admit that they rarely think about God, that they left the Church after confirmation, or that they are still carrying a deposit of anger towards God and the Church over a specific issue, most usually a divorce, sexuality issues, or even a poorly conducted funeral or baptism. We are always amazed how easily people will give up an important part of life because of the inadequacies of clergy, church policy, or boredom. At mid-life we are given the opportunity to renew or to accept the importance of the spiritual world once again. We feel that many people are frightened at the prospect of dealing with these global issues because they remind us that we are finite, that we live briefly and die, that life is difficult, and even more difficult at times to read any sense into.

By denying the existence of God or the use of a spiritual per-spective, people are able to stave off examining these quite dis-concerting concerns. However, they cannot be put off forever, and earlier in our discussion of existential *angst* it was made clear that this state is often the uncomfortable resting place for those who choose not to believe. And we do believe that it is a choice. Some of the most impressive men and women we have encountered in our work are those whose lives are described by a constant struggle and dialogue with a God who they do not experience at any meaningful level other than as an intellectual concept. However, philosophical theologians like Don Cupitt present a Christian 'non-realism' that is helpful to many modern Christ-ians. Cupitt suggests that a contemporary theology might be seen not as a description of objective reality – what actually happened – but as a 'guiding vision and programme for building a commu-nal world'. He continues in his introduction of the new edition of *The Sea of Faith*:

> The religion we have received seems exhausted. It spends its time boringly recycling a fixed canon of truth. But from the first there was the dream of a post-religious religion, a religion of creativity through which human beings might at last achieve the emanci-pation of which they have so long dreamt. Now, perhaps, cultural developments point to the possible emergence of such a religion. It will be a form of radical humanism.

While Cupitt's views are useful to those who cannot accept tra-ditional Christianity, the danger is that the power and beauty of Scripture can be ignored. We would argue that the so-called myths of the Bible and the life of Jesus act as powerful agents in forming the dialogue with God. However, in mid-life it is for each person to choose which path to take on their spiritual journey. Some will choose orthodox Christianity with its reliance of traditional language, liturgy and images of God while others will be more comfortable with a 'non-realist' acceptance of the way such language and images function in our spiritual lives, which is not to describe the relationship of humanity to an outside divine world but to articulate central truths between human beings. The central issue is, however, that what is missing in many people's lives is a means of making access to the life of the spirit. In mid-life listening to one's own inner voice is a beginning of what can be a process which leads men and women into this dialogue.

One of the most disconcerting aspects which we, as mid-life people, have to face in society is the changing culture which surrounds us. Today's world is not the same one we were born into, and the political changes alone are enough to cause confusion and anxiety. We were born before the concept of the Third World existed, the last vestiges of the colonial empires were just beginning to dissolve, and the United Kingdom was essentially an Anglo-Saxon bastion. None of this is true as we enter middle age, we now live in a pluralistic culture which is in the throes of self-definition. In our schools religious education has taken on a new meaning, and quite rightly people from non-Christian faith traditions are not satisfied with a one-sided Western Christian approach. For many of us this is difficult as we see our children learning less and less about Christian traditions and more and more about other world religions. Slowly but surely, the Establishment is being chipped away; there are now schools which follow the model of Church Aided Anglicanism but come from Muslim, Jewish and other faith traditions. These all present challenges to our faith, and as we enter mid-life we are forced into evaluating our spirituality in the context of a multi-faith society. These factors contribute to the anxiety which many men and women feel as they enter the mid-life negotiation and a common response is to retreat into what we know. Most of us are more than willing for people of other faiths to live in and to be a full part of society, but there is a tendency to want their cultural and spiritual values to be kept among themselves. As with many issues in mid-life when we know what we believe and what we value, we can gain a new confidence which allows us to relax our prejudices and entertain the possibility of being enriched by other people's religious beliefs. This is not a plea for the blending of all religions into one great understanding of God, but it is possible in mid-life to honour other traditions without giving up the importance and centrality of traditional Christian belief in our lives. The process is one of listening to other people's faith journeys, comparing them with our own, affirming the qualities within both which are common, and allowing room for contradictions. The result, almost always, is a strengthening and clarifying of our own spirituality, and we come away with a deepened understanding of God.

All of what has been discussed in the chapter could be summarized as a description of forging a renewed relationship with God based on our inner knowledge and experience. The voice which exists inside all of us is there for us to make use of, and mid-life is one of those special times when circumstance and process come together to offer us a conduit to that voice. That is one of special qualities of mid-life which is to be celebrated rather than feared. In the first stage of our lives, this inner voice is often denied its hearing because our life agendas cannot make room for it. When we are seeking someone with whom to share love, endeavouring to establish a career, searching for adventure and experience and exploring our sexual needs it is almost impossible to pause and listen to the message of the inner world. It is the rare man or woman who in the first stage of life is in touch with the inner life, and perhaps that is quite right. Perhaps the work of the first stage cannot be completed when listening to what Rilke calls God's song. Or perhaps it is rather that in the second stage of life we are able to hear the entire concert rather than just one voice at a time. In mid-life the choir invites us to look towards one another for love, growth and support rather than only to our own resources. The concert is one which takes all parts of life and blends them together to make a symphony. It is by listening to that symphony with the leisure of the perspective that mid-life provides that we are to be able to make use of it in forming our future.

5

SEXUALITY

God, I love sex! There I've said it. I'm terrified at the thought of having to give up sex since my husband died. I lie awake at night thinking that I'd give anything to have someone beside me ... just anyone to make love to me, to hold me. It's taken me a long time to admit that, and in fact, it took me a long time to admit that I liked sex a lot. We didn't have such a happy marriage, and lots of people end up idealizing their spouse when they're dead. There's not much chance of that with me. Nigel could be a real sod and sometimes I thought I'd chosen the wrong man for my life. Lots of times I thought about leaving him when things got really bad, but there were the kids ... and there was the sex. When he died last June, I was sad but we had been growing apart for years, and I can say that I wasn't devastated. I'm more devastated about being forty-five and on my own. Three months after the funeral an old friend came round for dinner. Scott was someone I had known for years and his marriage broke up about ten years ago; he's never really settled down since then. I must have known what was on his mind, lonely widow and all that, but I didn't resist. He ended up spending the night and the next morning when he left I felt absolutely bereft ... and that's why I'm here talking to you. I don't love him, I don't even care if I see him again unless we can sleep together, but that next morning I realized that sex had disappeared from my life. Each year as I get older and older, the chances of me having a sexual relationship decrease drastically, and I'm beginning to realize what that will mean for me. Do I just try to forget about it and take up a hobby ... that's a joke, I haven't found a hobby yet that's quite like sex.

77

At forty-five Janice is just beginning to understand and to accept her sexual needs, and this is not an uncommon mid-life scenario. For this woman it was the death of her husband that brought her sexuality into focus and under examination. For others it will be the natural ageing process, a divorce, our children's sexuality, or even the increasing pressures exerted upon us by a highly sexualized society. Our sexual identities are set early in life, and recent research in the States implies that sexuality may even be genetically determined. The discovery of the so-called 'gay chromosome' hit the headlines on both sides of the Atlantic last year, and perhaps the most interesting aspect of the discussion is the concept that what we previously saw as learned behaviour or preference might be beyond our control. For many gay men and women this comes as good news, relieving them of feelings of guilt and the often agonizing struggle to change their sexual identity. However, for most of us heterosexuality is the norm and we fit comfortably somewhere in the spectrum of sexual activity accepted and affirmed by contemporary society. At the same time our attitudes towards sex are set by family environment and the first sexual experiences of adolescence. It is at this time that powerful social forces come together to determine how much sex we have, with whom we have it, and the role it will play in our lives. For a woman like Janice, it is quite clear that sex is an important component of her life, and the prospect of losing it is frightening. Others may have less need or desire for sexual activity and find that while it is enjoyable it is not a central part of their lives.

One of the problems of mid-life marriage is that sexual desire often wanes for a period of time just when the opportunity for more privacy and intimacy increases as children mature and leave home. All of us know at some level, whether we can verbalize it or not, how important sex is for us, and acceptance of this is an important part of mid-life negotiation. If we have not done so earlier, perhaps mid-life is a most appropriate time to examine our sexual desires and to explore how they have influenced our lives in the past and will continue to do so in the future. An interesting private exercise is to sit down and remember our first sexual experiences, moving on through our lives until the present moment. Important questions can be posed at this point which can help reveal a sexual map for our futures. When did we first experience sexual feelings? Who and what were the circumstances of our first sexual experiences? What is most important aspect of sex for us: the orgasm, the intimacy, the cuddling and touching, the excitement and passion? What has been the pattern, or map, of sex in our long-term relationships or marriage? These are just a few of the questions which will get one started on this particular mid-life journey, and others will present themselves as we progress. An important aspect of this type of exercise is that it is completely personal, private and individual. There is no need to share this with anyone else, and of course it will lead us into closer touch with our own individuality. No two people are alike when it comes to sex, and people who have had many sexual partners attest to the fact that it is a rare thing to find someone who satisfies all our sexual needs, i.e. the perfect lover. Most of us integrate sex into relationship and there are many factors which affect sexual pleasure in long-term relationships. The danger when thinking about sex is to split it off from other parts of our lives and to see it as a separate sphere of activity. By taking sex outside of relationship we can place an unwarranted focus on the nuts and bolts of sexual acts: the who, the place, the behaviours, the rituals. One of the important challenges of mid-life is to locate the excitement of sex and intimacy within the context of our relationships as it is all too easy to fall into the trap of fantasizing about sexual activity which is not connected to our daily lives.

Christians have always had problems with sexuality. The Church's emphasis on marriage and family life can be seen from one point of view as a means of controlling sexual activity. This need for control speaks of the power of sex in people's lives and the perceived dangers of unregulated sexual contacts. Sex is not often spoken of in Christian communities and leaders of faith communities are cast in superior moral leadership roles when it comes to sex, although this is regularly seen to be inappropriate as they are men and women just like the rest of us. The popular media delights in stories about gay vicars or vicars who have sexual affairs with parishioners, treating the situations with an air of surprise and moral outrage that these people dare to be human like the rest of us. Robert Morely in his very good book on marriage entitled *Intimate Strangers* says: 'Sexual relationships in the West are characterized by guilt, and the sexual lives of public figures are subject to the sniggering obscenity of newspaper gossip-columnists in which we all share because of our own degraded view of sexuality'.

At its best the Church is ambivalent about sex, and at its worst it is prescriptive and moralistic; however, neither position is particularly helpful to those of us negotiating a mid-life change. The difficulty often comes from traditional theology which asserts that Jesus was both fully human and fully divine which would mean that he must have understood and experienced sexual desire in much the same way as we do. However, we have little guidance in the New Testament about sexual matters and we have to examine the texts more closely to determine how sexuality is to be integrated into our lives. If we proceed from the belief that God created humans with sexual desires and that one of the goals of the Christian life is to achieve our full potential as human beings, then it is appropriate to accept sex as an important component in the process. Sex is one of the most important means by which we can express our love for one another when we are in relationship, and we must accept that this is just what God desires for us. Therefore, an acceptance of our sexuality and our sexual needs is central to our growth as Christians. If this has not been done in the first stage of our lives, then mid-life presents another opportunity for creative growth.

One of the surprising results of this process can be an understanding of the changing nature of sexuality and sexual desire. This can be quite threatening as it challenges our sense of self. If our sexual needs are changing does this mean that we are not the same person as before? The answer, of course, is that we are not the same people as before; personality, sexual needs, values, priorities all change and grow as we grow, and it is in mid-life that this is often understood for the first time. Two aspects of the changing nature of sexuality will be dealt with later in this chapter and these surround the complex issues of sexual identity. Some men and women come to understand that part of their mid-life growth is the acceptance of their homosexuality and move into same-sex relationships. This is always a difficult process and one which their families find particularly threatening, but since an integral part of the mid-life journey is the movement towards an understanding and acceptance of our true natures it is sometimes a necessary and appropriate move. Other mid-life men and women find that they experience a renewed interest in sex and look for ways to express that interest. The accepted wisdom is that men engage in infidelity and that women become bitter and vindictive towards their partners. However couples do experience some difficulty around sexual issues in mid-life, but as stated earlier, one study shows that less than 2 per cent of men have more than one current sexual partner. The sexual challenges in mid-life relationships are around the discovery of an appropriate expression of sexual needs, acceptance of these needs being different in mid-life, and an acceptance of the physical changes which affect sexuality.

One of the factors which compound the difficulty of dealing with sexuality in mid-life is the emphasis placed on youth and youthful sexuality in contemporary culture. As has been noted earlier, we live in an increasingly sexualized society and are surrounded by media images of youth and beauty. These two elements are central to the marketing of almost every product offered to consumers, and our popular entertainment reflects this as well. The image presented to us is one which subliminally states that to be desirable is to be young; youth culture is pervasive and this often leaves the mid-lifer feeling left out and past her or his sell-by date. The reaction to these pressures in mid-life can take many forms with which we are all familiar: the man who parts his hair below his ears and sweeps it over his expanding bald spot, the woman who squeezes into a bikini on holiday and feels humiliated on the beach, the couple which take up a youth-oriented hobby and, of course, the enormous sales in beauty products to mask the ageing process. The goal for mid-life is an acceptance of the beauty given at this stage. This beauty is not one of youth, *naïveté*, or potential but rather one grounded in experience, survival and the joy of life's challenges. Of course, mid-life beauty is often enhanced by the ingredient of wisdom based on the experience of pain and loss which is always denied

81

the young. An anecdote will illustrate the confidence and beauty which can come with mid-life. Roy is a fifty-two-year-old solicitor who is often told that he doesn't look his age.

> I get so cross at the ageism inherent in these supposed compliments. I am not particularly good looking but I do keep myself fit and have always had an interest in how I dress. My life is quite good now that I'm over fifty; the first thirty-five years were a real struggle both professionally and personally, and my mid-life change was difficult because I was so unwilling to face up to the losses I was experiencing. However, I'm through that now, or at least I'm in a better part of the journey and I feel good about myself ... and that shows in how I look and dress. So, when people say, 'Gosh Roy, you don't look fifty-two!', I catch them up quickly by asking them what fifty-two is supposed to look like. Then I tell them this is how fifty-two is supposed to be and that I worked damn hard to get here ... I hope it makes them think a bit.

It is a fact that we will seldom be as sexually active in mid-life as we were in the first stage of life, and there are good reasons for this. Men and women reach their peak of sexual desire in their late teens and early twenties, and biologically this makes sense: It is at this time that most people have children, and our bodies are striving to perpetuate the race. Although today it is possible to delay having children until the late thirties or even into the fourth decade of life, most people listen to their bodies and the pressures of society in the first stage of life. What is left in relationships when the job of procreation is over, and what role does sex play in the relationship? For most couples sex becomes a means of expressing and deepening the sharing, understanding and intimacy within the relationship and takes on new meaning when sexual activity is not focused on having children. Sexual activity, its frequency and quality, can be a barometer of the health of any relationship. It is almost a cliché to say that if sex has disappeared from a relationship then the couple is in trouble. Like most clichés, there is a lot of truth contained in it which is founded on experience. However, there can be physical changes which affect sexual activity. For mid-life men and women menopause, prostate problems, breast cancer and hormone replacement therapy are all facts of life. While these problems do affect our sexual desire and activity they by no means preclude the possibility of sex in the relationship. The important thing to take on board when faced with a physical condition like those mentioned is that it will not define who we are as people. The condition may affect our life in some ways, but couples who are willing to face the implications of these mid-life problems can integrate them into a full life together, and this will include sexual expression.

The fear of impotence for mid-life men is a real issue, and one which can affect sexual expression. For some men the ability to maintain an erection can be affected by physical conditions, but in the main the emotional issues of loss and change as we enter mid-life have far more effect. It is important to realize that the fear of impotence is as debilitating as the actual problem itself. For sexually active mid-lifers there are definite worries as well about conceiving another child at a time when we are renegotiating our goals and renewing our inner lives. A new child can make important changes in this process, and the worry about giving birth to a handicapped infant will affect our decisions too. It is all too common for couples to relax using birth control as their sexual activity decreases, and the resulting pregnancy will influence our mid-life renegotiation dramatically. An important aspect of dealing with physical changes is a full understanding of one's physical condition and a frank discussion of it with both doctor and partner. This will help to relieve the fears which surround so much of mid-life illness, and when partners face the changes together the relationship is inevitably deepened.

For mid-life people one of the surprising discoveries is the arrogance of the young and those in the first stage of life. It is not surprising to hear young people express disbelief that their parents have sex, and the idea that men and women enjoy sex at all stages of their life is even more astounding to them. Recently a popular television comedy programme which is set in a retirement home featured several segments which dealt with sex between the residents who are all well into their seventies. The main characters not only reminisce about their past sexual experiences but discuss the possibility of sleeping together. When the family and directors of the home find the two in bed together the disbelief, disgust and outrage they express reflects quite accurately what society in general feels about sex and older people. The question then is: is there sex after forty . . . or fifty . . . or sixty . . . or even well into old age? The answer is a resounding: 'of course; and it's quite natural'.

This is not the sex of the first stage of life which can be described by its intensity, frequency, and power as well as being filled with a sense of wonder and discovery. During marriage counselling interviews in the 1950s and 1960s a common example given to couples when discussing sex was the famous peas in a jug story. It went this way: if you put a pea in a jug every time you have sex in the first two years of marriage, and then take a pea out every time you have sex after that it will take a decade to empty the jug. The amusing thing about this story is that this is what passed for sexual counselling in marriage preparation in the past, and it is also amusing in its underlying assumption that sexual activity in a partnership will automatically decrease as the marriage continues. There is some truth in this, but experience shows that it is a poor example as sex is more about quality than quantity. Sexual expression in mid-life has its own special qualities, and these are qualities which can only be gained from experience and time. Many mature men and women have had the time to explore and to define their sexual needs, and they have also had the experience to know how to please their partner as well as themselves. When two people are in a long-term relationship the stability and confidence which that relationship engenders allows each partner to explore the world and to pursue new opportunities. This can be a time of extreme creativity, but the danger is that the very stability of a long-term relationship can be seen as stifling and limiting. Let's look at Sandy and Linda talking about their marriage when they came to counselling in their mid-fifties.

> There was never any doubt that we loved one another; we've been married over thirty years and they have been good years overall. We are nothing special, just an average middle-class couple: three children, a small mortgage, two fairly successful careers, and a dog. We sailed through our thirties and forties

without the upheavals that our friends were experiencing and felt quite proud that we didn't divorce and that our children turned out rather well. Both sets of our parents died within five years and that was difficult for us; we began to see that we were the next generation and that we would die before too long. I guess we began to realize that we had more time behind us than in front of us. Strangely enough we began to look at our marriage, and especially our sex lives, when the issue of the ordination of women came up at church. That may seem odd, but we were both violently opposed to the change and fought it out on the PCC. We heard speakers from both sides and some of the women deacons who came to speak impressed us, and one of them pointed out that it wasn't the young people or the older people in congregations that opposed the ordination of women, but middle-aged people like us.

'I began to think', says Linda,

was I one of those spoilers who couldn't look at any issue without harkening back to the past? These women really made me think about myself rather than about them, and I began to wonder what I was trying to protect. It was really about myself, not women priests. I realized that I was afraid of any changes in my life, that I never complained about the way things were because I was afraid of what change might bring for me personally. It didn't take me long to begin looking at my marriage since that's the most important relationship in my life ... and I thought that I was missing something. One night I couldn't sleep and I got up and began going through the picture albums starting with our wedding. Before long I found myself crying for no reason which was odd because the pictures were all of happy times. I guess my crying awakened Sandy and he came downstairs and sat beside me on the couch. I tried to pass it off as hormones, but Sandy is a practical Scot and he wasn't having any of that.

When I came downstairs I was really knocked back when I found Linda in tears. I knew something was wrong, but she couldn't, or wouldn't, say what it was. Eventually I started flipping through the photos and I began to feel strangely sad too. I saw pictures of the family at the beach and I hardly recognized the two slim, young parents holding the children. Linda put her finger on her picture and asked me if that was the reason I didn't fancy her any more. At first I didn't understand, but then I twigged that she meant that she wasn't young any longer . . . and then I got really frightened. I don't much like talking about these things, and I felt that if we opened the door we might find things behind it that would change our lives forever. Then Linda said, 'It's been almost a year Sandy . . . a year since we made love', and then I got really scared.

We talked that night about our marriage and how slowly over the past five years sex had dropped out of our lives. Linda thought I wasn't interested any more or perhaps it was just natural for men to lose interest when they turned fifty or so. I realized that it had been going on for a long time, ever since the children went through puberty. Our kids were very active socially, lots of girlfriends around the house, and it seemed as they got more sexually active we got less and less interested in each other. In a way I think it was seeing them so young and vigorous that made me feel sapped of my energy and power; maybe that's why me and the boys had so many rows over how late they stayed out, what they were doing on weekends away and at parties. My boys were becoming sexy men and I was becoming an old man. I think I just gave up and it was then that I found myself on the conservative side of every issue in opposition to what my sons were thinking. This women priest thing was only the latest in lots of changes that we both tried to resist . . . I guess any change was too dangerous.

'That's why we came to counselling', says Linda.

Or rather that's part of the reason but most of all I felt trapped since the children left. I realized that I had never made a readjustment to life when I stopped being a full-time mother. Asking questions about what you want to do with the rest of your life is frightening because you might not want to know the answers. When I let myself do this I came to understand that I wanted my life to be with Sandy, but I wanted it different. I knew we couldn't have back the excitement we had when we were first building a life together . . . or the exciting sex for that matter. But I thought with all the years we have invested in one another there must be some way to move through these feelings of emptiness. So we decided that night to be brave and to do things we had never done before to see if they would help. We didn't see ourselves as 'counselling people' so that in itself was a change. We may have been stuck in our ways and afraid of change, but we did know what we wanted if we were going to change: some sex in our lives to go along with the intimacy which we had already, a way through the angry feelings we experienced about the world moving along without us, some new shared goals for the life in front of us . . . and a bit of adventure and excitement.

Sandy and Linda are unusual in that they came to counselling for positive reasons; they didn't feel their marriage was in immediate danger, just dying on the vine. Theirs was a courage born out of desperation at the prospect of losing something which had been central to their lives, their marriage. Their initial response to mid-life was to try to stop change at all possible costs. They wanted to defy time, hold back change, in order to convince themselves that life was not slipping by. Rather than bending with time, mourning their loses, and moving on to new possibilities, they presented a rock wall of resistance and the only way through a rock wall is to break it apart. The wall began to crumble when Sandy and Linda's children left home and what they found behind that wall was a marriage in deep trouble. The most disturbing aspect of what brought the couple to counselling was the lack of sex in their relationship, and this is even more common than we realize.

Most couples are faced with an important decision in mid-life and that is whether to renew their relationship, accept it as it is, or leave the relationship to be alone or to seek another. If the choice is to renew, what can be built is a relationship, accept it as it is, or leave the relationship to be alone or to seek another. If the choice is to renew, what can be built is a relationship based on the acceptance of our partners as the people they have become rather than as the people they were in the first stage of life. Usually this takes the form of accepting that our partners are just as human as

87

we are and that the marriage can continue based on love, friendship and companionship. From this basis a renewed relationship of equals can be forged whose form can be dictated by the needs of the two partners. Many therapists are currently under fire for assuming that all middle-aged women carry around vast amounts of unexpressed anger and that the best way to deal with that anger is to leave their partners and to be alone. While this may be sound advice for some, especially for those in physically and/or emotionally abusive relationships, we feel that the courageous option for most couples is renewal. Of course, the cost of renewal is often great, both in time and emotional resources; and it is much more glamorous to envision a life of freedom and personal growth while living alone. The reality is often much more bleak as mid-life men and women find it quite difficult to re-enter the social and dating world. Evidence of this is shown in the tremendous growth in dating agencies and in the past ten years the appearance of such organizations specifically for Christians. The alternative is the hard work of rebuilding the lines of communication which have disappeared over the years and this must begin with a commitment to honesty. Let's examine the process as experienced by Sandy and Linda.

A major problem which surfaced in their counselling was the fact that they were both Christians and actively involved in congregational life. Since their presenting problem was lack of sexual activity, it soon became apparent that the permission to discuss sexual matters was tacitly withheld within Christian communities. As stated earlier, the Church is at best ambivalent about sexuality and there seems to be little encouragement to discuss sexual activity as an integral part of mid-life marriages. Sandy eventually was able to acknowledge that his decreasing interest in sex had a lot to do with a fear of impotence. He cited a few instances when he had not been able to maintain an erection and rather than suffer the humiliation of this he withdrew from initiating sex with Linda. This distancing made Linda feel undesirable, and as she began to notice the ageing process she assumed that Sandy was no longer attracted to her middle-aged body. In their counselling there was a moment of tender humour when Linda expressed her sense that Sandy no longer found her attractive. Sandy shifted in his chair, blushed, and leaned towards his wife. 'You musn't think that love. Sometimes when I see you getting ready for bed I think what a beautiful woman you are and what a podgy slob I've become. That's why I always wait for you to turn out the light before putting on my pyjamas. How could you fancy this body ... even when I can get hard enough to be of any use to you?' Linda leaned towards Sandy and touching his fly said, 'Sandy, that's the least interesting bit of you I want ... although it's quite interesting when it's on offer'.

This very intimate and telling anecdote indicates the safety which both partners felt throughout the counselling process. The counsellor was able to provide very safe boundaries for the couple and because of this Sandy and Linda could express their feelings openly and with humour. One of the gifts of mid-life marriage can be the discovery of humour based on many years of shared relationship and a growing sense of one's own self. The novelist Maggie Gee has written sensitively about mid-life in several of her books, most recently in her novel *Lost Children* where she tells the story of a woman facing mid-life renegotiation. In a newspaper interview Ms Gee spoke about her own perception of the gifts of the ageing process.

> One of the worst things about being young is that you think everything is your fault, and it's such hard work. The great thing about being middle aged is that you stop thinking everything is about you. You realise that, in fact, practically nothing is. That the reason the ticket collector was so dreadfully rude had nothing to do with your face, it's just that he was having a bad day. And that friend who rang off as soon as you rang was merely having a row with her husband. What a relief it is.

Accepting that the world does not centre around us is an important step in mid-life renegotiation and one which often occurs in the area of sexual relationships. Linda began to see that Sandy was struggling with his own set of fears and inadequacies and that many times she had mistaken his fear of sexual inadequacy for lack of attraction to her. Together they worked with their counsellor to renew their relationship and to accept both the new gifts and new limitations of middle age.

This discussion of sexuality within permanent relationships would not be complete without addressing the subject of infidelity and the implications of it in mid-life. Infidelity is almost always the symptom of a much deeper problem which is not being faced than it is a solution to a relationship which is not working. Earlier we said that a recent study reported that only 2 per cent of the men surveyed had more than one current sexual relationship, and the figure is even lower for women. If this is true, then our image of the philandering mid-life man or middle-aged woman with her 'toy boy' is a myth. While it certainly occurs it may be its uniqueness which attracts our attention. It is also well to keep in mind that the popular media on both sides of the Atlantic have an obsession with the sexual lives of celebrities and political figures. This is bound to skew our perception of the frequency of infidelity. While casual sexual affairs are almost always damaging to both parties in a marriage or permanent relationship, they most usually have little to do with sex. This may sound strange to the reader but the point is that while the sex in an affair may be good the affair itself can be seen as an attempt to work through other problems. These problems for mid-life people often centre around feeling trapped in a dull, routine domestic life and a search for new challenges and excitement. Too often men and women feel that this excitement cannot be generated from an existing mature relationship and that starting again is the only answer. A particularly dangerous aspect of mid-life affairs for men is the ironic fact that it is often the success and power in their professional lives which attract younger women. It is easy for men who were not socially successful in the first stage of life or sexually attractive to women at that time to mistake the attentions of younger women as a response to them as sexual beings. If they lose their power or position they most often lose the younger women as well. However, it is even more damaging if a man comes to realize that it is not his 'self' which is attractive but what he has and can continue to produce in the form of money, position and power. The authors have seen too many men, and some women as well, leave a long-term marriage for a younger partner only to replace it with a slightly altered version of what they had. Listen to Kevin.

I was bored with my wife and our children were almost grown up when I met Maria. She was twenty years younger than me and I was flattered that I could still 'pull' beautiful women at forty-five. The sex was good for a while but then it became routine, but still nice. Eventually Maria wanted to settle down and I envisioned travelling, going to the theatre, and an active social life like I had twenty years previously. Her friends were young and exciting and they treated me like I was something special. So I did it, and now it's ten years on. Last Sunday I took my four-year-old daughter by Maria to the Christmas panto accompanied by my twenty-year-old son from my first marriage. I now have two kids at college, one in university, a four-year-old who takes all my spare time and Maria wants another. You see, my twenty-five-year-old sex goddess grew up and wanted to become a wife, mother and career woman. I feel like I've come full circle and the circle is narrowing every day; I'm now fifty-five.

Kevin now realizes that he merely exchanged one traditional relationship for another. At the time of his mid-life renegotiation he lacked the courage or vision to face his problems of boredom and fear of ageing within the context of his then current marriage. Had he done so, he still may well have ended his marriage but now he will never know. The encouraging aspect of this story is that Kevin shared these feelings at his first counselling session with his therapist and Maria. It is not possible to change the past but we can change the future regardless of from where we are starting. For women the issues are often different and they centre around an experience of emptiness at mid-life expressed by the 'Is this it?' feeling. For women this process often starts when children leave home or when they realize that their partner has become dull and uninteresting to them. More and more we are seeing women who, like Kevin, feel that they are losing their sexual attractiveness, and if they have not developed careers or other creative outlets, they will be condemned to a life of family routine characterized by feelings of missing the best part of life. It is not surprising to learn that mid-life women are the largest group diagnosed and mistakenly treated for depression in this country.

It is still a fact that physical attractiveness is more important for women than men despite the influence of feminism in the late twentieth century. One of the interesting side effects of hormone replacement therapy (HRT) for mid-life menopausal women is that they often report renewed sexual energy. This newfound desire for sex can challenge their partner's virility and sexual performance thereby bringing new tensions to the relationship. HRT also can restore energy and self-assertiveness and promote a creative and vibrant mid-life beauty. Physical beauty is still a primary tool for attracting men and when that begins to fade so can a woman's confidence. For women, beauty is connected with youthfulness and as we all know youth fades quickly. The American author Susan Sontag says, 'Women become sexually ineligible much earlier than men. . . . Most men experience getting older with regret, apprehension, but most women experience it even more painfully: with shame. Ageing is a man's destiny, something that must happen because he is a human being. For a woman, ageing is not only her destiny . . . it is also her vulnerability.'

A woman, and many gay men as well, can experience the loss of sexual attractiveness as a sense of becoming invisible. Gay men are included here because gay lifestyle emphasizes youth and beauty and middle-aged gay men often share the same feelings on this issue as their feminine counterparts. Both groups say that they are demoted in rank from possible sexual partner to the more mundane generic category of 'middle-aged person'. This fact was brought home to one of the authors while working on this book. During dinner at a smart London restaurant the handsome young Italian waiter was attentive and professional, but when he served younger people at nearby tables we noticed he chatted in a relaxed manner, offered suggestions about ordering food, and eyed up the young women at the table. A woman at our table wanted more coffee and couldn't get the waiter's attention: 'He doesn't see us . . . in more ways than one!', the woman said. 'We don't exist for him. We are just old people eating dinner, not real human beings. I've noticed this the last year so it must mean I'm middle-aged now. The hurtful thing though is that I *want* the waiter to notice me; I'm not ready for the scrap heap just yet . . . somehow or other I feel that I might end up as one of those pathetic older women making a fool out of herself over some young stud just to prove a point.' A sexual affair which contains elements of romance and secretiveness is often used as an anecdote to a dull life or to the aforementioned invisibility. Most mid-lifers will remember Mrs Robinson from the 1967 film *The Graduate* and the famous Simon and Garfunkel song. To escape her desperately dull marriage and crass husband Mrs Robinson seduces her daughter's suitor, and it is she who is left wounded and alone at the upbeat happy ending while the two young people flee the confines of middle-class life. Mrs Robinson is pictured as the pathetic victim of her own lust, but examined from a mid-life perspective she is a woman who uses the incorrect tool for managing her mid-life renegotiation. However, it must be acknowledged that sexual affairs have a tremendous attractiveness and power as well as the ability to delude us into feeling that we have found an easy answer to a complex problem. The heady mix of desire, secretiveness, and the forbidden unite to convince us that we are different from others who have tried this solution and that we will be the one who is actually renewed and in some way reborn by the affair. Mid-life affairs are always a call to an inner examination, and this examination must be both spiritual and emotional as what men and women are expressing is the death of the spirit in their current relationship. New Testament Scripture has little to say about marriage but it does have a good deal to say about forgiveness, reconciliation and renewed life through accepting our brokeness before proceeding to growth.

Age difference in relationships presents unique problems for the older, and usually mid-life, partner. Kevin is now fifty-five and Maria is thirty-five; while he is thinking of retirement and accepting the limitations of a physically deteriorating body she is still an active and vibrant woman. When these relationships begin the age difference is usually discounted by the partners saying that it doesn't matter to them, or the older partner doesn't act his or her age, or even that the younger partner looks forward to caring for the other in their 'golden years'. These are brave words which almost always prove not to be true. What is more common is impatience and resentment on the part of the younger partner as they realize they are bound to someone whose physical abilities are dramatically different from their own and whose worldview begins to focus more on winding down and accepting life as it is rather than looking for new challenges. Health complications in ageing partners can exacerbate problems in the relationship and the romantic dream of caring for a handsome older man becomes a grim nightmare. Older partners in these relationships often panic when the age gap becomes more clearly visible and feel insecure that they may lose their lover to someone younger. This can result in increased possessiveness and dependency which predictably drives the other partner away. Other older partners will attempt to deny their age by dressing in young fashions, taking up punishing exercise programmes to tone their middle-aged bodies, or more negatively by retreating into depression or drink. These issues must be handled sensitively and honestly by those in age different relationships, and it is important to find activities and a social and family life which suits both partner's needs. It is necessary to acknowledge what it is that both partners bring to the relationship as ageing occurs and that the need for reassurance and affirmation may be more important for these couples than for others where there is little age difference.

Another common problem which is expressed by younger partners is the fear of being left alone when their lover dies. This often occurs in their own mid-life and compounds the normal difficulties of the grieving process. Just when other couples begin to renegotiate their future life together these partners face a mid-life without the support of someone they have loved for many years. It does not help that they knew this when entering the relationship and the challenge is to rebuild a new life on the foundation laid by the old. The problems of age different relationships are much the same for gay men and women, but they must face them without the support and acknowledgement of society. While today there are more tolerant attitudes towards gay men and lesbians there is little of the complex social network which supports heterosexual couples. In many situations the younger partner must face their problems or even the loss of a partner without the support of their families or co-workers. Age different relationships are quite common among gay men and many of them are long lasting and fulfilling for both partners. When a gay man is in his forties or fifties it can be a social asset and a mark of his continuing virility to have a younger partner, often twenty or even thirty years younger. The younger man gains the stability and maturity offered by the older and these relationships are not the exploitative model often characterized in novels and in the media. However, no matter how loving and supportive of one another, the partners do face mid-life problems. If the relationship ends the older man is often left truly alone, unable to compete in a highly sexualized and youth-orientated sub-culture. For the younger men the death of an older partner places them back in a social world limited by the spectre of HIV/AIDS and one with which they may no longer be familiar.

The issue of sexual identity is a difficult one in our society and as has been mentioned earlier in this chapter new research is suggesting the possibility of genetic factors being as important as the socialization process. Regardless of what we choose to believe about how sexual identity is determined, the fact remains that some mid-life men and women experience a change in the expression of their sexuality. Another important fact is that many homosexual men marry for social reasons or in order to have a family: even the most honest and open of these types of marriages are not without their tensions and the couples involved almost always say that they did not realize how difficult it would be. While this can be a fulfilling life for some, others will experience tremendous inner pressure to realize their homosexual desires which they may have hidden from their partner. For men this usually results in anonymous, secret sexual encounters in public toilets, in parks, or one-night stands while travelling. The authors feel that the duplicity and lack of integrity that this kind of activity engenders can only result in emotional damage to the individual and to the eventual destruction of any marriage or long-term heterosexual relationship in which they are involved, often with disastrous results for the family.

Women have a different experience of their sexuality and many women who enter lesbian relationships while married do so to escape marital abuse and subjugation by men. They often make a conscious decision not to relate to men sexually and seek women for comfort, support and understanding as well as sexual expression. But this is not so for married men who acknowledge homosexual desires or have sex with men. They speak of their sexual feelings as the 'true' part of their nature which they have to suppress to be accepted by society. The authors have never heard a gay man who has been married say that he left his marriage to escape domination or abuse by women, even though they may have experience of both. This is a difficult process for anyone who has denied their sexual desires for the same sex for such a long time, and one which must be faced with courage and compassion by all those involved. The authors hesitate to recommend counselling as an immediate response to all mid-life problems, but this is one area where we do advocate it; individual counselling and sessions with the current partner are almost mandatory to avoid unnecessary pain and long-term emotional damage. One of the few Christians to acknowledge the reality of the mid-life sexual identity crisis is the Bishop of Bath and Wells, The Right Reverend Jim Thompson, in his autobiography *Half Way*. Bishop Jim says that he has come to realize that it is appropriate for men and women who have been suppressing their homosexual desires to come to terms with them in mid-life. For some this will be an acknowledgement and acceptance and a choice to remain in their marriages. Of course for others, the only course is to end their heterosexual relationship, and this is often a difficult and angry process. In Scott Turow's novel, *Pleading Guilty*, the author depicts a husband's confusion and pain at learning that his wife is having a lesbian relationship and that she has always had relationships with other women.

> She apparently did not consider that it wasn't particularly easy for me. People stay married, who hold on for the long pull, put up with a lot from each other: personal oddities, bad habits, ill health. For some it's tolerance, others commitment, many, like me, fear the unknown. For a while I tested myself with the notion that I should put up with this too. People stay married without sex. I'd known plenty. After all, I grew up Catholic. And who ever said it had to be like that? But it just sort of cut to the heart of things. I never saw this issue in normative terms. I wasn't worried that it was a perversion, or something that would have made my sainted ma faint, and I gave Nora no points just because it was the

latest in style. It just seemed like an awful lot not to know. For her not to tell. For me not to recognize.

However, it can be the first step on the road to a life of integrity as our sexuality is central to who we are as human beings. Sadly the reality for individuals facing this decision is that they can expect little support from the Church, and there are few, if any, useful public role models for men and women who acknowledge their homosexuality in mid-life. The work must be done by the individual and this is the reason that counselling is essential to the process as it is inevitably filled with fear, anger and a sense of loss which needs to be untangled gently so a renewed and more authentic life can be born.

A special sense of loss can be experienced by single people as they enter the mid-life renegotiation. Some singles will have chosen not to marry and may have had a fulfilling sexual life based on uncommitted relationships. They will face similar losses in mid-life to those who find themselves single at mid-life through the death of a partner or divorce. Other single people may have never had sex in their lives and can experience deep pain at having been denied this important part of human experience. It can be especially difficult to enter mid-life and face the fact that they will never have children and most likely will never experience a sexual relationship. For all singles, however, the opportunity for sexual expression diminishes greatly in mid-life as they are not able to compete with those who are younger, and this is especially true for single women.

Society often assumes that single men and women, and especially those who are Christian, do not have a sex life or even sexual desires. This 'desexualization' of singles hinders the mid-life adjustment as there are few places to turn for support. Sonia is a woman who did not marry but talks about two great loves in her life, one with a man who she chose not to marry and one with a married man.

I'm fifty-five now and I've come to accept that I may not have sex again before I die. This sounds depressing and in some sense it is because I enjoyed the sexual relationships in my life. I'm very glad I didn't marry Rolf though I loved him. We would have been very wrong for one another and we both see that now. We still keep in touch and he is happily married with grown children. We were too much alike and he suffered from a type of existential depression in his twenties which I found keenly attractive and seductive. Our life together would have been a disaster, so I feel that I did a very courageous thing. My other great love occurred when I was well into my thirties while doing some retraining work. The sex between us was the best I've experienced in my life and the sharing was deep and fulfilling. I had no desire to break his marriage though he would have if I had asked. I will always carry the sadness of our love, but I do have the experience to keep with me. For me it was a process of letting go of my sexual desires while at the same time not giving them up. I am still attractive and I may well meet someone with whom I want to begin a relationship. I haven't shut off the possibility, only the likelihood. This has released me to pursue other non-sexual relationships which fulfil me in different ways. The last bit of counselling I gave myself centred on this area and was useful as I was beginning to panic about the future. Living alone, it is easy to dwell on what one doesn't have rather than celebrating all that is there in my life. I would never say 'At least I had two important sexual, romantic relationships' as if they were two lovely paintings that have been destroyed. These two loves are part of me and I realize that they continue to form me as a woman and empower me for the future.

This chapter opened with a mid-life woman acknowledging her need and desire for sexual expression . . . 'God, I love sex'. Perhaps that is an appropriate way to close it as well. For Christians sexual relationships offer the opportunity for a unique understanding of the gifts given to us in this life. Adrian Thatcher, in *Liberating Sex*, understands the God-giveness of sexual relationships when he says:

> Christian faith acknowledges relationships as belonging to the very heart of God. God's nature is love, and this nature has become known to Christians in what became called 'Persons' – Father, Son and Spirit. . . . In remaking us as sexual beings, God, through the Holy Spirit, gives us the power and the vision to

make relationships which resemble those relationships existing eternally with God.

6

DEATH AND LOSS

I'm a classic mid-life person of my generation. Born just at the end of the war and raised during a time of incredible prosperity, I think I must have hit all the great social trends of the past fifty years. I remember James Dean and Marilyn Monroe; Sex, Drugs and Rock & Roll mean something to me, I remember the Summer of Love and spent a few years as a pseudo-hippie, and I gave it all up for a house, home and family in the seventies. However, I don't think I began to grow up until my two-year-old daughter asked me a question which is still with me today as I enter my fifties: 'Mum are you going to die? Am I going to die?' The anxious look of the little girl so afraid that the answer would be what she feared the most still plagues my waking dreams today even though she is twenty-five. My answer was that we would all die someday, but not for a long, long time and that it was nothing to worry about now. What a lie; I worry about it all the time and especially since I turned forty.

Christine, the mother speaking in the interview above, lives with the heightened knowledge that life is finite and she is still struggling to deal with the inevitability of death. It is a particular irony that we only know we live because we understand that we will die. Dorothy Rowe, in *Time On Our Side*, says:

If no one ever died, if we all lived for ever, we would not know that we were alive. We have the concept of life only because there is death. Part of coming to terms is accepting the presence of death in our lives, and recognizing its importance. This means recognizing that everyone will die and that there are no exceptions, recognizing that the process cannot be prettified or glossed over no matter how we might try, and recognizing how death can show us what is actually important in our lives.

This leads us to an existential understanding of life and death for if we live for ever what can matter; any decision, any choice, we make is just as valid as any other. However, in life as we know it, decisions are what gives existence meaning and importance. This is basic to our humanity and is what gives us a personal sense of meaning. In mid-life we are called to listen to our inner voice and to begin a dialogue on the meaning of life for the time we have left becomes precious to us. It is at this time that many of us come to realize that we are mortal for the first time as the arrogance of youth is stripped away by the ageing process. This can be an exciting time for the challenges come from within us, and it is by meeting these challenges and making decisions for the future that we begin to live the second stage of our lives.

For many of us the catalyst for this dialogue is the death of our parents. Even if our parents have died before we reach mid-life the experience is still with us as we begin to realize that we will die soon as well. This is often too overwhelming to accept at once and for many it will take months or years to negotiate this last step towards freedom. The term freedom is used because one cannot truly be free to make choices about one's life until death is accepted. At some time or another we all believe that we are immortal and that we will be the one who lives forever. This belief is an unconscious defence against the existential terror at the thought of the end of life. In a previous chapter Alvin spoke about the ennui that brought him back to therapy many months after his own father's death, and this is a common mid-life experience. At mid-life the acceptance of death can rush in upon us with disabling force, leaving us with the surety that time is running out. This can be an intense period as it is often combined with children leaving home and the feeling that one is alone is heightened. Questions asked at this time take the form of setting goals for the future: 'Will the next half of my life be worthwhile?' The answers to such questions take the form of a dialogue with the inner self, and this is essentially a spiritual dialogue whether one is a practising Christian or not.

Alistar came for bereavement counselling even though his father had died while he was an infant during the war. At fifty-two, Alistar had just experienced a set-back in his work and felt guilty that he had let down some of his teaching colleagues in Scotland. He came saying he didn't understand why he was feeling so sad lately; so sad in fact that he found himself crying at work or on the way home on the train. Over several sessions Alistar began to dialogue with the lost father he had never known and with his own sense of being cheated and abandoned almost before birth. He came to understand that he had always felt alone and that his attachment to institutions came from his desire to belong. This combined with a need to take care of others, especially protecting the underdog, had formed the basis for his teaching career. In mid-life when a community education project he had been managing was summarily closed he felt unnecessarily responsible, taking all the blame on himself. Whenever he would speak of his colleagues and the position in which they were left after the closure of the project, he would begin crying. In time Alistar understood that he was crying not only for them but for himself, for his life which had been typified by loss and loneliness. Since his mother had withheld the details of his father's war record and death and only grudgingly leaked a few of the facts, he had no clear picture of the man he called father. The next step for Alistar was to search out the past which had been denied to him and eventually he found his father's grave in Normandy. He also found that his father had been a complex personality and that his rebellious tendencies brought him to volunteer early in the war before conscription was mandatory. His mother had been harbouring some resentment over this for years and felt that Alistar's father's heroic behaviour during the war did not justify what she saw as his earlier abandonment of the family. Alistar was to learn that his father died while leading a voluntary patrol on a dangerous mission behind enemy lines. Rather than focus on the glamour of his father's death, Alistar identified with his bravery and ability to lead and to care for others, characteristics which Alistar saw in his own life.

The reclamation of his father gave Alistar not only the courage to accept that he was alone, but also the courage to look for

102

meaning, challenge and quality in the second part of his life. Eventually he was able to abandon his guilt over the closure of the project and to work towards an acceptance of his ambivalent relationship with institutions. He loved the security and sense of belonging which came from working in a bureaucracy while at the same time such a system gave him a convenient paternal figure against which to react, something which he lacked in early life. His reputation as a 'maverick' manager had kept him at the front line of education middle management but allowed him to go no further. Alistar decided he wanted to work in a more nurturing, co-operative environment and eventually moved into private charity work where he now directs a charitable trust. In a smaller organization he found the challenge and opportunity for quality work which was lacking in his local education authority job. His energy returned and he continued the second stage of his life with new meaning and purpose. While Alistar's mid-life journey may sound easy when seen here on the printed page, it took several months to reach the point where he understood the appropriate content of the dialogue suggested by his inner voice. When this had been accomplished, the agenda set, he moved quite quickly in processing the feelings and his depression lifted with rapidity. There are always ways and means to escape the existential bind of the immortal-mortal tension presented by life, but the path is rarely without challenge and pain. One of the interesting aspects of mid-life renegotiation is that we are almost always equipped to handle the work if we can find the appropriate companion for the journey. It is not always a counsellor, it does not always take months or years, but it does take courage and the strength to perform an act of will in choosing to begin the dialogue.

The danger in a book like this is that if only success stories are presented the reader begins to feel that the work of mid-life is simply accomplished if they follow the recipe given in the text. Negotiating mid-life change is often a difficult process typified by periods of growth and regression. Some men and women may work quite slowly and the mid-life renegotiation can take several years. Others will never really complete the process and their lives will contain a slow progression towards only some small sense of fulfilment in the second stage of life. This is sad and quite painful; however, as has been said over and over again by the authors, growth in mid-life often demands a courageous act of will. Someone who has not been able to perform this act of will, and therefore has struggled through mid-life fighting the demons of depression, ennui, and loneliness, is Wilfred. Now in his early sixties, he has been struggling with his mid-life renegotiation for almost a decade. For many years Wilfred took care of his invalid mother and it was only after her death that he found the courage to begin the difficult task of building meaningful and deep personal relationships. After finishing university he rose quickly in the field of medical research where his detachment and gifts of insight and discernment were valued. Wilfred never married and was not able to form long-term relationships which included sex. His sex life was characterized by casual affairs, usually while on holiday or travelling on business. As an only child and a high flyer academically he never developed adequate social skills and was terrified at the prospect of trusting someone in a deep way. For most of his life Wilfred concentrated his energy in his work and in being a dutiful son to demanding parents and when his mother died he was near the top of his profession. It was at this point that Wilfred began his much-delayed mid-life renegotiation. For all his life he had suffered from depression and debilitating migraines which would keep him off work for days at a time. His suppressed anger at the unfair aspects of his life came out in his social contacts as well, where he was noted for his acerbic wit.

Although people were drawn to his intelligence and sophistication they were repelled by what they saw as his negative view of life and often vicious attacks on people whom he didn't respect. By the time he was fifty, Wilfred confessed that he had many people in his life whom he had known for a long time, but very few, if any, people he could count as friends. At various times in his life he considered counselling or advice from clergy, but he could not bring himself to begin the process of opening himself to and trusting another person. He refused to discuss his parents and their influence on his life as he idealized their family life, and Wilfred also feared the judgement of others so much that he denied himself the opportunity for a fuller life because the emotional risk was too great. In addition, the qualities which made himself successful in his professional life disabled him in his personal life: he had the intelligence and sophistication to know intellectually where many of his problems lay, but lacked the courage to confront them. He kept himself in a state of tension caught between wanting to change and fearing the price of change; the result was depression, suppressed anger, migraine headaches and deep feelings of loneliness.

Slowly after his mother's death he began tentative forays into the world of feeling. Initially he accepted a lodger who became a friend. As the lodger did not come from his professional or social world, Wilfred was able to practise being the person he might like to become. The relationship deepened and Wilfred was encouraged to expand his social life and to consider counselling. He also began to make use of his new friends by sharing his feelings, asking their opinions and sometimes taking their advice. A pattern of growth began to emerge: he would introduce a subject for discussion such as 'Counselling is useless; you only hear what you want anyway', then he would destroy his opponent's arguments, and later he would take some of what was said as useful and act on it. This was a tedious process for the friends involved, but Wilfred was able to begin building relationships of trust where people were able to tolerate and to enjoy his idiosyncrasies. This pattern has continued for a decade and Wilfred is a happier person, more in touch with his anger and those fears inside him which keep him from people, and he has made some changes in his life; however, the growth has been slow. His depression is more transitory now, but his migraines still plague him. Wilfred's main area of growth was in the development of personal relationships and he now has several deep friendships with men he can trust. He is able to give loyalty, support and sometimes love to his new friends, but his is a sad story because Wilfred is a man of immense gifts and unrealized potential, especially in the important areas of caring for others and allowing them to care in return. He is a man who cannot bring himself to listen to his inner voice which calls him to reach out in love and to ask for love; and if he were reading this now he would say, 'That's ridiculous; you can't possibly speak that kind of romantic clap-trap about human beings. It's just not useful'.

We have seen how death plays an important role in mid-life, working as a catalyst for change and also as a herald of our mortality; but there are special issues for men and women experiencing mid-life renegotiation as well. One of the special issues is the death of a child which can bring enormous problems to a mid-life marriage. Mid-life is also the time when some of our friends begin to die. For gay men the experience of having friends die of AIDS is now common and it is not unusual for many gay men to have several friends who have died or will die of HIV/AIDS-related illness. Mid-life can also bring the onset of some chronic diseases or life-threatening illnesses and clearly this will influence the decisions we make for our lives in their second half. There are many reasons why parents may outlive their child but the most common are cancer, accidents and lately HIV/AIDS. Marriage and relationship counsellors tell us that many marriages do not survive the death of a child due to the feelings of anger and guilt experienced by both partners. This kind of death also brings to the surface many problems which may not have been acknowledged in the past by mutual agreement. When these issues combine with the abnormal pressure of the grieving process for a child the focus for the negative feelings is often placed into the relationship. Symbolically letting go of the relationship can be used as a means of letting go of the pain and grief caused by the death. In mid-life we may well be questioning the person we were and drafting an image of the person we may want to become, and the emotional devastation brought by a child's death intensifies the interior examination, often with damaging results.

One of the real difficulties of dealing with the emotions during this time is that this kind of death is so 'unnatural'; we are meant to die before our children – that is the way human existence is constructed. Much of the joy and satisfaction in mid-life for parents comes from seeing their children mature as adults and sharing as grandparents. Many men and women see their children as the one lasting accomplishment they will leave behind for even the most celebrated are forgotten within a few generations. From the point of view of the biologist this is quite true as

106

it is our only opportunity to contribute to and affect the gene pool for future generations. For people of faith the death of a child can challenge their faith and understanding of the ultimate meaning of life. When a child dies people usually react quite strongly to the pastoral care they are given, either negatively or positively. It is common to place one's anger and frustration on the representative of God and to be oversensitive to any small mistakes or omissions the clergyperson may make. If the advice given in normal deaths is not to make any major changes for at least a year, the advice in this situation should be doubled or trebled. Again, this is one of the few situations which seem to demand counselling, often both individual and with one's partner. It is all too easy to retreat into self-destructive introspection and emotional withdrawal. Bereavement counselling and support groups are an excellent means for managing the feelings of this type of loss.

For gay men in mid-life the implications revolving around the issue of HIV/AIDS deaths are complex ones as they involve our sexual identity. Ageing, as has been discussed, is a difficult problem in the gay sub-culture, and the constant reminder of mortality and the precarious health status of many of one's friends contributes to any feelings of despondency and hopelessness already present in mid-life. There is also the issue of guilt in the gay community for those who are healthy. Samuel is a sixty-year-old gay man who has many younger friends who are HIV positive or have AIDS-related illnesses. After a young friend died of an HIV/AIDS-related illness he spoke about his feelings.

> Most of my friends are younger, in their thirties and forties, and I worry about their health. In some ways they see me as a parent figure, and since I have trouble making friends it's an easy role to play. But I do feel left out since so many of them seem to be HIV positive; I can understand their worries and problems but it is difficult for me to empathize because I'm one of the lucky ones. And I do mean lucky because I've done all the things they have done and there is no real reason why I should not be HIV positive as well. When Jeremy died I was consumed in the caring process during the last few months and helped organize the funeral as well. As I'm older I was the liaison with his mother who visited

for the last few weeks from the States. When it was all over and his mother went back to America I felt unusually depressed and it didn't lift. I kept wondering why it was him and not me; I know this is a common reaction but it was really quite strong. A few weeks later for no reason at all I went for another HIV test and it was negative as I expected. The worrying thing is that I was disappointed.

In the area of HIV/AIDS the global and spiritual issues are quite confusing and the process of identification with those who have died can be quite strong. Samuel has found a nurturing set of friends only to have that security threatened by random death. The fairness issue is quite important and it is easy to feel that someone in mid-life should by rights be a more appropriate target for illness. The other difficulty which Samuel faces is that he knows that the issue will not be resolved because he lives, and is in relationship, with a group of friends who know their health will deteriorate and that they will most likely die before him. This omnipresent sense of death, loss and the need constantly to let go or not to hold on too close to those we love works to destabilize our emotional balance. More than any other group, mid-life gay men need mutually to support one another in these difficult situations as there seems to be no early solution to controlling the virus or the onset of HIV/AIDS-related illness. This can be done both formally and informally through group process, but more simply by talking about issues and confronting feelings. For the mid-life gay man there is an immediacy about the mid-life renegotiation process as they have a foreshortened sense of time. One of the goals may well be to live more in the present and not to delay making useful changes in life; this can be a highly positive result from the epidemic.

Of all the losses and adjustments in mid-life, coming to terms with death in whatever form it takes is easily the most difficult work we have to do. The work must be done on several levels of experience and this makes the process complex. From philosophical theologians like Tillich to the anthropological psychologies of Freud and Jung, there is agreement that a personal integration of death into our living present must be negotiated before we continue into the second stage of life. One of the challenges which our own death and the death of others present to us is the opportunity to let go of what has gone before. That is not to say that we forget our past and those people who have moved through our lives, but rather that we hold them close in our hearts as quiet companions for the mid-life journey. The events and people of the past are no longer with us and we musn't betray their memories by making them present in our lives in the form of anxiety, depression or unexpressed anger. It is all too easy and cowardly to use those we loved who are dead as tools for refusing to move forward. That is the true work of mid-life, moving forward as reborn people, not frozen between the outer directed goals of the first stage of life but accepting the call to inner growth. A large part of that inner growth will be measured by our ability to see life as a series of small deaths and losses and to accept this as the natural cycle of life rather than raging against the unchangeable reality of life.

When a partner dies we cannot escape the fact of our own mortality, and our grieving is greatly influenced by this sense of the fragility of our own life. It is dishonest to say otherwise, and when the poet, John Donne, says that any man's death diminishes us, the truth which lies beneath that statement is more personal that we might admit. As we stand next to the coffin of our partner, child, mother, or father we begin to realize how much and how quickly life can change. Through relationships we bind ourselves to the present and often use our domestic routine to hold existential questions at a distance, but when someone close dies this distance is shortened and we are brought into dialogue with death. This is one of the events in our lives which will convince us that we are truly alone. Part of the denial process in life is convincing ourselves that through intimate, often frenetic involvement with life, we are immortal. One of the attractions of living our lives like a soap opera, moving from one dramatic trauma or exciting accomplishment to the next, is that it helps support the idea that we will live for ever. We must be immortal if we experience life so intensely, and the intensity of daily life blocks out any intimations that life will end. We are so busy moving from one drama to another that we begin to believe that life will always continue in this way, and that we will continue along with it. This fantasy is quickly shattered when someone close to us dies and we usually attempt to integrate the death into our soap opera although it is rarely part of our original script.

During the time of the funeral, death is our constant companion and it is interesting that we have invented rituals to move through the grieving process and to begin life once again. One of the great gifts of organized religion are these rituals and those who do not make full use of the Church or their religious institution at this time must depend on their own individual resources. The rituals, the visit from the vicar, the funeral service, the funeral gathering which follows, visits by friends and relatives, all carry some of the burden of the pain of death for us, and without them some will collapse as the existential distance between their daily lives and the knowledge of their own mortality is erased. It is easy to reject the wisdom of the Church in these matters as we forget that Christians have over 2,000 years of experience in dealing with death and tend to locate Christian tradition in the current practice and personality of the local church and its vicar. Most Christian ministers understand that at this time they are both themselves and representative of a larger and more ancient process of confronting death and moving back into life. The movement back into life after the death of a partner is an important rebirth and begins when the funeral is finished. Like many of the rituals in life, if we examine them closely we see the rhythm which undergirds our existence: birth, death, renewal. We live and love our partner, death comes and we are thrown into the acknowledgement of the fragility of life and the reality of separation and pain, then we are invited to live again but as a new creation. We are given the choice: retreat or advance. For those who enjoined the mid-life journey there is no choice but to advance.

Much has been, and will be, said about renewal and rebirth in the mid-life renegotiation process and the freedom which this renewal brings in the second stage of life. Nothing contributes to this goal more than accepting one's own death. At mid-life our parents die, some of our friends begin to die as well, and this is an invitation to look inside ourselves and to integrate death into our lives so that we may live fully in the future. It is possible to reject this invitation, and it is possible to say to life as Peter O'Connor phrases it, 'that one does not wish to take on life as a development rather than a fixation, that one is not prepared to see it as a series of deaths and rebirths, that one is really not up to the fullness of the journey and would prefer to tarry awhile in the known and comfortable'. Andy speaks for many of us when he talks about coming to terms with his mortality. He is a mid-life man who describes his first stage of life as a being obsessed by a desperate denial of his own mortality, a denial which limited and controlled his choices and experience.

I was very close to my mother who was a very damaged woman although she had many great gifts and strengths. She was terrified of death and I was raised in a home full of superstition, good luck charms, and one where we existed only in the present. I remember that neither my mother nor father ever told me about death and I only learned that we did not live for ever when I was sent off to Sunday School. I could not believe it and refused to accept the possibility that my parents, as well as myself, would cease to exist at some point in time, and my mother told me not to have morbid thoughts and to forget about it. That's exactly what I did not do; I was obsessed with death denial for over forty years and I cannot remember one day when it did not enter my consciousness. When my daughter was born I was in the delivery room and the doctor was impressed with the tears that were streaming down my face. What he assumed were tears of joy at seeing life begin were in actuality tears of pain and despair at knowing that I would some day lose this child through my own death or that she could be taken from me by her own death. In some ways I'm surprised that I even allowed myself to marry and have children as my sense of possible loss was so present with me.

Throughout my life I've had secret small rituals to ward off death: I would hold my breath when crossing a bridge, if I began to have thoughts about death I would make a fist and tap my knee until the thoughts went away, I never looked at funeral processions, graveyards, or attended any funeral service. This was my secret and of course I would never talk about death with anyone, and if the subject came up I would absent myself emotionally from what was being said. The implications for my life were profound. Part of me wanted a life of travel and adventure as well as deep relationships with people. Because of my obsession with loss and death, I would not fly. I could not bear the thought of being away from the security of my normal domestic routine. For a partner I chose an emotionally distant woman so that I would not care too much and for friends I chose those who needed me more than I needed them. In that way I would have no fear of losing them.

All this came to an abrupt crisis, not when my parents died as you might think, but when my daughter was born. I was in my late thirties at that time as I had delayed until the last moment the decision to have children. While there was a good deal of joy in the birth I was soon after thrown into frightening panic attacks followed by bouts of depression. I felt tortured by the possibility of losing my child and she slept next to our bed in a cot for over a year. It was not uncommon for me to stay awake for hours watching her to make sure she didn't stop breathing. I know this all sounds quite mad, and it was. My daughter's presence in my life brought me to a confrontation with the feelings that had been trapping me into a life of anxiety and ritual obsession. I was so afraid that I would damage her life by transmitting my own fears to her that I entered counselling without much hope for success.

That was over fifteen years ago and I'm amazed at the progress I've made. I look back on that person who was so trapped and controlled by his fear of death that he wasn't living life, only trying to avoid the inevitable. My counsellor and I began gently as I was so frightened by even talking about death that I would hyperventilate at just the thought. Eventually I came to understand what it was that I feared and how that was controlling me. I began to see that choice only had meaning in the context of a finite life. If I have only two hours for dinner in a restaurant I must chose something from the menu before the time is up. If I wait to the last minute to chose my starter there's no time for a main course and certainly no time for dessert. I was able to extend this simple analogy to life and eventually to my life and realize that my life could then have meaning. The beginning was my choice, along with my wife, to have a child. That choice led me to the understanding that I could tolerate the paradox of life and that life could contain dignity and worth rather that fear and anger. My love for my daughter and the fear of damaging her gave me the courage to begin my mid-life renegotiation. The good news is that somehow the pain of accepting my mortality has made me understand and appreciate the beauty and possibilities contained in the life I've been given. My spiritual life has deepened tremendously during this time, not as a promise of something better in the next life. I'd like to believe in an afterlife but for me I find it might be a dangerous trap to displace my hope; it's much healthier for me to leave that up to God and to trust in the love given by him in this life . . . I'll just have to wait and see. What I do know is that my life has been renewed by accepting death . . . paradox again. . . . I now fly with only minor anxiety, my daughter is allowed the freedom to be her own person, and my life has begun to take on meaning.

The fear of death and the control which that fear can exert over our lives is often a spiritual issue. Andy has moved to a renewed relationship with life and God by accepting the fact of his own mortality, a process which has been difficult and long. For many Christians, especially those with traditional beliefs, there is a tendency to avoid talking about death or to feel guilty about their own fears and anxieties about an afterlife. A literarist belief almost demands a full-scale acceptance of heaven and hell as places of punishment and reward. If so then Christians should be pleased that their loved ones are reunited with God. This attitude can bring on feelings of guilt when the anger and pain of loss must be suppressed. It does not serve ourselves or God to avoid these feelings regardless of what our theological construct of afterlife looks like. Perhaps more devastating for Christians is the all-too-common experience of losing one's faith during a time of bereavement. When dealing with loss the feelings of abandonment and emptiness often suggest questions about the existence of God, even for practising Christians. Rather than finding solace in Scripture and comfort in the pastoral support system of the

Church, it is just as common to feel alienated and angry. At this time it can feel as if the security of a relationship with God has been robbed from us by our experience of loss. The promises inherent in the Christian tradition can appear empty and meaningless, and we can feel as if we have been duped. Psychologically it is a means of projecting our unacceptable feelings on to another object thereby releasing in some sense our own pain. This distancing might be healthy for a time, but for men and women in mid-life who have been Christians for a long period of time the discipline of returning to services, prayer and Scripture is an important process in renewing their faith. Often the sense of alienation and emptiness will remain for a considerable period, but by placing ourselves physically within the context of God's presence this can eventually be released. The important thing to remember is that God is the depository of all our deepest feelings, and even the most dangerous and painful feelings are not unacceptable to him. When facing issues of death and loss Scripture is an important tool for unlocking the secrets of our hearts and facing the terror of our own mortality.

Divorce and separation are not issues which one might expect to be included in a discussion of death and loss; however, it is important to acknowledge the death of a relationship and the losses attached to that death. It is all too easy to move out of what has been a long-term relationship and into another without stopping to examine the cause for the breakdown. Although divorce is not as common in mid-life as is reported – most marriages end within the first ten years – it does occur frequently. The ending of a relationship is often a reflection of dissatisfaction with the path our lives are following, and it is not the relationship which is the cause of the problems. Again, it is easy to mistake the symptom for the disease. The 'dis-ease' is an uneasiness with our life as it has been lived in the first stage. Divorce and separation can be the first call to an inner examination and renegotiation of a different set of goals for the second stage of life. It is not the shedding of a partner that is the important work here, but the acknowledgement of deeper issues. The first step is the understanding and acceptance that there have been both good and bad elements to the relationship and a search for any elements which

114

might continue to play a part in our lives. Many divorced people become good friends only after the separation. There are churches which provide services for the ending of a relationship and these can give a formal structure to provide psychological boundaries for the painful separating of two lives. A bereavement process which works towards a realization of the loss when a relationship ends can be the beginning point for renewal.

Renewal is also an issue for single people when their parents die. In our society singles often find that they do not fit comfortably into the coupled environment of mid-life and many have found their sense of identity and security in relationship with their parents. The early childhood identification with parents continues well into mid-life for them, and the bonding can be quite deep. When the parental relationship between parent and child continues into mid-life, it is difficult to escape the sense that we are still children with all the support that knowing one's parents are always there to provide. Some singles may have not established an independent life, living physically with parents for all their lives. When the parents die, an important part of their inner life dies as well. The mid-life renegotiation process can begin with unexpected suddenness and it is easy to feel overwhelmed by feelings of loss and abandonment. Depending on the emotional skills which the person possesses, the process is often difficult and the tendency is to form another attachment similar to the parental one in emotional structure. The courageous single can use this seminal loss as a catalyst for determining who they might be as an independent person and begin to build a separate and new identity for themselves.

Death and loss are difficult issues for all men and women in mid-life especially since the prospect seems more possible or imminent than ever before due to the ageing process and the intrusion of death into our lives. However, it can be a time for creative restructuring of our lives and goals and is often the first call from our inner voice for re-examination of our lives. The process is not an easy one or one which can be accomplished quickly as has been seen by the men and women whose stories have been shared in this chapter. Perhaps the last word on death and loss and the hard work which needs to be done if we are to live abundantly in mid-life should be left to Carl Jung, whose own mid-life renegotiation when he withdrew to the shores of Lake Zurich makes useful reading. He says, 'The serious problems of life, however, are never fully solved. If ever they should appear to be so, it is a sure sign that something has been lost. The meaning and purpose of a problem seems to lie not in its solution, but in our working at it incessantly'.

7

THE CHANGING SELF

May God bless and keep you always,
May all your wishes all come true,
May you always do for others, and let others do for you,
May you build a ladder to the stars and climb on every rung,
And may you stay forever young.

This is not the authors jollying the reader along with false wishes
for eternal youth; it's the first verse of a popular song written by
Bob Dylan which the famous, and still popular, singer/political
activist Joan Baez sings for her rapidly maturing son. Recently Ms
Baez, who is now in her fifties, filled a London concert hall for
several nights to sing songs which made her famous and new
ones which tell about her life journey. She came on stage wearing
jeans and a white shirt tucked in at the waist to flatter her still
slim figure and congratulated the audience for being there and
congratulated herself for still being around. As she stood there
with a stylish short cut to her distinctly greying hair, the wrinkles
in her once perfect skin were highlighted by the spotlight; the
auditorium broke into spontaneous applause to tell the performer
that she was loved, that she was still a role model for millions of
mid-lifers, and that she looked good. Most of the audience was
made up of men and women in their forties and fifties who
seemed to be looking for a bit of nostalgia and an affirmation that
it was alright to be over forty and still vital and alive. Ms Baez
could easily be the role model they were looking for as she is still
clearly enjoying her life, looking good without the aid of cos-
metics or face lifts, taking on new challenges and causes, and
dressing the way that she feels is right for her lifestyle. Later in the

evening she sang a new song, 'Speaking of Dreams', about her current relationship with a much younger man who she credits for waking her from the doldrums of mid-life. 'You were not even born yet when I began my career in '59 . . .' and the house roared with approval.

What the mainly middle-aged audience was applauding that night was the life force still active in the performer and her ability to project into song the vitality and energy which she experiences in her life. The song she sang for her son, 'Forever Young', is not about eternal youth but rather about an integrated acceptance of what life brings and an acceptance of the movement of time. These two elements, combined with a sense of personal integrity, can guarantee that we will retain the vitality of our younger selves, not youth itself. What a contrast this woman is to others of her generation who seem to be setting a trend to deny the ageing process! Cosmetic surgery is spoken about proudly on American talk shows which fill our afternoon television, Sunday supplements feature cleverly retouched picture stories about glamorous, sexy women in their fifties and sixties, and most recently there has been much controversy about women in mid-life still bearing children through artificial means. All this would lead us to believe that as a society we are not only terrified of ageing but even more terrified of looking old. Perhaps in a consumerist media-dominated society, like Great Britain is rapidly becoming, this will be seen as the only last true sin. Across the Atlantic from all appearances this is already true. If this is the case, then we are in real trouble . . . because the mirror doesn't lie.

Each morning we are faced with the reality of the ageing process. As we lift the stubbly grey cheeks, or try to whip our thinning hair into a youthful style, or reach for the pot of eye gel which is guaranteed to reduce the crows feet, we are reminded that we are no longer young. One of the problems for most men and women in mid-life is that there is a disparity between the way they look and the way they feel. We may look middle aged but most of us feel much the same as we always did, sometimes full of life and at other times tired after a good day's work. In working with people in mid-life transition it is quite common for them to talk about their parents' ageing process and to make connections with their own. Diana nursed her mother for the last year of her life and it was a time when the two became close in a way they had never been before. The eighty-two-year-old mother, although physically dependent on her forty-year-old daughter, enjoyed her life until the end, and her physical limitations gave the two time to know one another in a deepened way.

Mother didn't sleep much the last few months and we would sit up and watch television and share a bottle of wine until the wee hours. I would sit opposite and look at the little shrunken person my large vibrant Italian mother had become and wonder what it was like for her . . . being so old and so infirm. One evening I think the wine really got to us and I introduced the topic of how she felt about being old. My Mum always had a sharp tongue and she replied, 'How do you think it feels? How would you like someone wiping your bum just like you used to do for them when they were a toddler?' And she laughed and asked me if I seriously wanted to know. Of course I did and she continued by telling me how strange it had been for her during the past few months since she couldn't take care of herself. Somehow she never really believed she was old until then, even though she could see and feel the changes in her body. 'In my mind, Diana, I still feel twenty-five or thirty, I think I always have. When I was in my forties I noticed that people started treating me differently, with more respect, especially the girls in the shops and the young men at the grocery. I thought it was amusing because I didn't feel any differently. Then when you kids got to be teenagers you used to talk about the two of us as if we were fossils; we used to laugh about it. You all were so arrogant and sure of yourselves. Again, I took it as a joke because my mind hadn't aged – I mean there weren't any changes to the way I thought about life or people – only my body was changing. After that the wrinkles came fast and furious, I sort of let myself go physically, but not mentally. Even when I got to be seventy I was often caught off guard because someone made an assumption about what I would think or feel because of my age, and I would get offended that they couldn't see the person that was inside me.' I now know what mother was talking about as I move into my mid-forties and lots of my friends feel the same way. It's a bit frightening and sometimes I think that I should fight the wrinkles and fat and that this would somehow maintain the balance between how I look and how I feel.

There are varying reactions to the ageing process which can range from unrealistic denial and a desperate search for lost youth to total despair and resignation. Diana took strength from her mother and attempted to meet her ageing in a positive manner by seeking to value the advantages of mid-life and to let go of what can no longer be. An opposite approach was exhibited by Lionel who found the ageing process disabling and destructive. While most men grudgingly accept the bulge appearing where their waist used to be and the loss of muscle tone, Lionel was deeply affected by the physical changes he experienced as he entered his forties. The influence of the fitness movement in this country is beginning to affect men of Lionel's generation who took their bodies for granted. While many see positive aspects to the interest in individual exercise programmes over team sports, there are elements of narcissism in the growth of fitness centre memberships and personal training programmes which the group of men now in their late twenties and early thirties will have to face in mid-life. Lionel is probably typical of many married men of his age; he had enjoyed team sports at school but, as he became involved in his career, opportunities for exercise seemed more difficult to find. By the time he was approaching forty the only exercise he found was the occasional game of tennis or a walk to the shop for the Sunday papers. This, added to the normal ageing process, brought Lionel to an abrupt realization that he was growing older when he injured himself getting off a bus.

> I just stepped off on to the pavement and my back went out. Suddenly I was down on my knees and I couldn't get up. The pain was excruciating, and even more humiliating than crouching there with my briefcase was that I had to be helped to my door by our next door neighbour who was returning from an OAP afternoon social club. It took me a week to get up off the sofa and my doctor was very encouraging. He said that back problems

were not unusual in unfit men of my age who lead a sedentary life and carried around a stone of extra weight. Well, that pretty much summed up my life, and I found the entire experience very depressing.

In fact Lionel marks his back incident as the beginning of the depression which brought him to counselling and in some ways marks the beginning of his mid-life renegotiation. His slowly decreasing physical potential became a symbol of the movement of life for Lionel and the periods of immobility brought on by his back problems allowed him to reflect on his accomplishments and goals. Lionel was particularly engaging due to his ability to stand back and observe his obsessions and laugh about them, but he was unable to manage the anxious feelings about his age and what the future might bring for him.

Of course the doctor advised me to lose weight and to get some exercise. The first time I went to the fitness centre I was given an evaluation by one of the instructors, a Greek god of twenty-five who kept saying, 'For a man your age you're not in too bad a shape'. His unconscious arrogance infuriated me and after the evaluation I scurried back to the changing room for my clothes and went home. For a month I didn't go back and I found myself avoiding the mirror in the morning or shop windows when I was out walking. I thought if I didn't concentrate on my body and just got on with my life the feelings I was experiencing would go away soon, but they didn't. I felt sad for no apparent reason – my life wasn't that bad – and I couldn't drag myself out of bed in the morning, although that was probably due to the fact that I was hardly sleeping. At one point during this time my wife was clearing out some cupboards and she was piling up some of the children's baby clothes to send off to the Christian Aid Fair at our church. I remember that I was so hurt by the idea that she wanted to throw these things away; I tried to convince her that we should save them for our grandchildren or that the children themselves might want them for momentos. She put a few things aside to save but packed the bulk of them for delivery and put them in the boot of the car. They are still there as I just couldn't bring myself to let go of them, so I just never got around to dropping them off.

Lionel's reaction to the passing on of his children's baby clothes became yet another symbol of his grieving for his past youth and the desire to hold on to it in the present. This process became so exhausting for him that his back problems increased and he spent more and more time at home sulking in bed. In counselling Lionel began to understand that he was experiencing a grieving process which is typical for many mid-life men and women; sadness at the loss of their youthful hopes and dreams both in the exterior and interior world. He was not willing to give up the past and couldn't move creatively into the future. Part of the problem for Lionel was that he did not realize exactly what had been lost as it was more than external achievement and changes in his physical appearance; these are simply windows through which we can look to see the actual loss, our sense of self. Lionel was at the beginning of the process of rebuilding a self that would be authentic for the middle of his life.

At the same time Lionel was experiencing change in his physical and emotional life, he found profound changes in his spiritual life as well. Men often experience an awakening of interest in spiritual matters which goes along with their call to an inner examination of their previous life experience. Many mid-life men and women of faith find that their relationship with God undergoes a change at this time but it is not always positive.

I stopped going to church; my back pain was the excuse as I couldn't sit for long on the hard pews at St Dunstan's. At least that was what I told myself and my family, but the real reason was that I found the services depressed me even more. For some reason the positive messages of Scripture didn't ring true for me any longer and I felt that I just couldn't believe them. I guess I lost my faith if you want to put it that way. To tell the truth, I was angry with God because I felt betrayed. I thought I had tried to live a Christian life and what was the reward? Depression, pain and emptiness. If that was the result of years of churchgoing then I didn't want any more of it. Our curate came round one evening for what I supposed was a pastoral visit; I had been off work for a few days with my back again. He's not a young man; in fact he's a good deal older than I am, but he's full of energy and he wouldn't take no for an answer when he suggested we go out for a drink. I limped off with him and we actually had a good talk; the first of many. Fr David has the same kind of sense of humour that I do, so I had to laugh when he asked if I was ready to forgive God for letting me get old and was I ready to let go of the 'Jack the Lad' image of myself that I loved so much? 'I know you're having trouble with your spiritual life but you don't have to let your spirit die, Lionel' was how he put it. We went on to talk about my feelings of depression and loss of hope for the future and he didn't try to chivy me out of my sadness.

Over the next few weeks I began to realize what an important time this was for me and I was able to gain some idea of how exciting it could be. I did feel like all the spirit had gone out of my life, but what I was facing was an opportunity to rebuild life in a new way from the inside out. That sounds like a tall order and it has been.

An important part of the mid-life process for Lionel was his need to mourn his losses and to let go of the person he had been in the first stage of life. Only when this is done are we able to greet the new person we are becoming. His desire to cling on to his children's baby clothes was a symbol of his own clinging to his boyhood dreams and fantasies, some of which he had been able to realize as an adult and some which needed to be gently put to rest with his youth. Lionel was clearly experiencing a call to examine his inner life at both an emotional and spiritual level, and it would have been more convenient for him to concentrate on the physical aspects of ageing by working on his body. However, he came to understand that without an inner examination and change no amount of physical exercise or transformation in physical appearance would accomplish the mid-life transition.

In the discovery of their authentic selves at mid-life, both Diana and Lionel were able to make use of individuals who could facilitate their change. For Diana it was her mother's wisdom and her counsellor's guidance, for Lionel it was his curate and his doctor. It is important that in mid-life we are sensitive to those who come into our lives at this time: many of these people can become important catalysts in mid-life renegotiation if we allow ourselves to make use of them. One model of understanding how God works in this world is the incarnational view that God is present in all of his creation, not by magical interventions when summoned up by prayer and fasting. The challenge for us is to integrate the wisdom of Scripture, the tradition of the Church and the world in which we live and move. The mistake of the secular-humanist is to confine human growth and potential to the life of the mind and the emotions and to ignore the life of the Spirit. They feel that the abuses of religion far outweigh its use in mid-life transition and seek to release people from their sense of guilt, depression and ennui by common sense and deep psychological examination. However, this is too simplistic and the popular psychological gurus often give recipes for growth and change which leave out an essential ingredient. It is much like attempting to make bread without the yeast: what you get resembles bread but it is quite flat and without the height, texture and quality of real bread. One of Jung's most famous statements concerns just this when he says that he had not met anyone who had made a successful mid-life adjustment who had not come to terms with the transcendent or metaphysical component of life. Peter O'Connor explains, 'By religious he did not mean anything to do with organized religion, but rather that the anima, or soul image, was in essence spiritual'.

In his book *Soul Friend* Kenneth Leech examines the concept of spiritual friendship which is often key to a mid-life transition. For Christian men and women entering a mid-life renegotiation this can be an important element in the process, finding someone to share the journey. In Lionel's life his curate became an important companion on his journey, and Fr David was able to share his own experience of life as an equal within the context of a shared Christian belief. It is important to understand that when looking for companions on our mid-life journeys we should be seeking relationships of reciprocity. Often the confusion and depression experienced at the onset of mid-life can push us towards seeking a guide or guru figure. For many this is a counsellor or therapist, for others it is a minister of religion. While the former is costly and good practitioners will refuse to become gurus, the latter are often only too eager to take on parishioners for counselling or spiritual guidance to feed their own unacknowledged desire for omnipotence and need for control. If this is the case, the result can be quite destructive for the mid-life man or woman as eventually they will learn that their guru is only human, whose only true gift is to be a companion along the mid-life journey. It is a much healthier model to discover those who are within our lives already who have potential for this relationship. This book is full of examples of men and women who have joined in strength with others who are experiencing mid-life growth. It is easy to discount the contribution which can be made by those who know us well or who have been in our lives for a long period of time. It is this richness of shared experience which often can lead both friends forward on the inner journey. At the same time it must be said that new friends can provide an important sounding board for our mid-life exploration and growth. Lionel and his curate, David, became friends and since they had little shared past experience they were able to approach one another without preconceived ideas of who one another should be. Lionel felt a freedom to share his deep feelings with David that he would not have experienced with someone who knew him well.

> David became a sounding board for me and vice versa. I would try out new ideas on him and he was able to give his opinion without any investment in what the result would be as he was not part of my day-to-day life. This was important to me because I felt so trapped by the expectations of my family, and quite frankly I was embarrassed to share some of my feelings about ageing with my wife or other friends. He had been through all the ageing stuff about ten years previously and I was surprised that he had felt much the same way. I guess you could call the relationship brotherly in the true sense of the word since I respected and grew to love David, but he remained very human and ordinary for me. There was no temptation to romanticize our friendship as he is such an ordinary guy; I think I give him as much as he gives me.

While Lionel and David were able to build a positive friendship which empowered both of them in the life journey, there will always be people in our lives who play an opposite role, a disempowering one, if we allow them. In these cases the courageous course of action is to let go of the tension and sometimes to let go of the relationships. Sandra discovered this in her marriage when she began to make positive changes in both her spiritual and emotional life. At forty Sandra decided to do something about her weight problem and she marks this decision as the beginning of a long period of mid-life transition. She had always been over-weight but in the previous decade she had become obese. Sandra's desire to lose weight came from the fact that she found it almost impossible to do her job as a social worker in the Mid-lands, and her opportunities for promotion were limited because she did not have the energy or appearance required. Her husband did not seem to mind and never pressed her to lose weight but was supportive when she would attempt to diet. Through her church Sandra entered a combined counselling/weight loss pro-gramme and did quite well although she often had to fight her husband's desire for splurges on pizza or sweets. As she lost more and more weight, she found him becoming impatient with the dietary routine and with her commitment to it. At the same time Sandra began to take on responsibility at church for Sunday School and for the co-ordinating of a parish visiting scheme. As she became more involved her husband withdrew from the activities they had shared previously and became increasingly critical of the time she spent outside of their home saying that she no longer cared for him or the life they had built together.

Sandra continues the story.

When I had lost about half the weight I wanted to, Jerry, my husband, encouraged me to stop. I thought I looked good, my energy had returned, and I generally felt a lot better so slowly I drifted away from the weight loss group. However, I kept up my activities at church and at work they were offering me a supervisor's job which would require me to do a good deal of travelling and co-ordination, something I had always wanted to do since we didn't have children to tie me down. Jerry was totally opposed to the idea and wanted our old life back. Slowly I began to listen to what he was saying and I realized that what he wanted was to be the centre of attention again. When I was obese I was his 'big mother' and that was most likely the reason we never had

children, not my weight problem. I suggested marriage counselling but Jerry didn't want anything to change; he wanted me back
the way I was, fat and nurturing. It would be nice to say that I
stood up for myself and demanded my own life, but I didn't have
the courage to listen to what I heard inside myself. We started
eating together like in the old days and soon I was even heavier
than before and to top it off I was put on medical leave from my
job against my wishes. What happened next I've heard called 'a
creative illness', but what I experienced was a gall bladder attack
which put me in the hospital. My doctor came round and said
how disappointed he was to see me in such a state. 'You're not
listening to what your body is saying to you Sandra', he said, but
I knew I wasn't listening to what my soul was saying to me. My
life in the church had brought me to understand that there are
many different levels of understanding and interpreting life's
journey and that for me the spiritual one was as important as any
other. I realized that my soul was crying out for change and that
listening to the voice inside me would mean that I could pursue a
different path in the second part of my life, one which was healthier both physically and emotionally. I desperately wanted Jerry to
join me on the journey, but he wanted what he had always known
. . . someone who could meet all his needs regardless of the cost to
them. I realized that he was willing to allow me to destroy myself
to save himself.

When Sandra left hospital she returned to her weight loss
regime and eventually accomplished her goal. Jerry found that he
couldn't love the person she had become and left soon after. It is
not surprising to learn that he remarried quite quickly, chosing
another overweight partner who would be bound to him in much
the same way as the 'old' Sandra had been. Jerry could not move
into the next stage of life, but hung on desperately to what he
knew. Sandra's story is dramatic and painful because to
accomplish her mid-life renegotiation she had to give up a good
deal – not just her marriage. Rather more important, in some
ways, was the fact that she had to give up the old image of herself
as unworthy of love. She had to give up the protective covering of
fat which shielded her symbolically from the world of feeling,

and she had to give up the habit of denying her inner needs to service those of others.

So far this chapter has dealt primarily with the painful aspects of the changing self, but there are physical gifts to be valued in mid-life as well. Someone who has negotiated the mid-life transition in a positive way often becomes very attractive to others due to their newfound confidence and goals for life. It is not surprising to learn that most counsellors and therapists are middle aged and that many people prefer to work with those who are. Younger therapists have a difficult time establishing a private practice and usually attach themselves to institutions or referral organizations. There are good reasons for this as when people are in pain they often look for a parental figure or wise guide as they feel that some of that person's personality integration may be transferred to them. This is deeply embedded in all cultures and more traditional cultures honour their older members in a way which we have lost in the West. There is a growing body of writing in this area focusing on the rediscovery of the lost fathers and mothers, which speaks of the need within us all for the discretion, understanding, experience and confidence which age can bring. There are some myths about sexuality in mid-life which it would be useful to explore, namely that middle-aged people lose their sexual attractiveness, their interest in sex and ability to be satisfactory sexual partners. While there is some truth in the fact that in our society we equate sexual attractiveness with youth this is not always the case. There are any number of older men who still come out in top places in the lists of celebrities women find appealing: Sean Connery, sixty-two; Richard Gere, well over fifty; and for the raunchier tastes Mick Jagger, fifty-plus. The reason for this is not necessarily their physical appearance – certainly Connery and Jagger are no beauties – but rather their air of confidence about their lives and what they do. When a man or woman has made the mid-life renegotiation in a positive way, in other words when they have grieved for the loses from the first stage of life and considered the possibilities for a positive future and then moved on courageously, the process is reflected in who they become. Paul, a fifty-plus gay man, speaks about his second stage of life.

One of the themes of my mid-life change or whatever you want to call it, was that I gave up competing on lots of different levels. I moved sideways in my job because the pressure to produce more and to outstrip younger colleagues was giving me an ulcer. This felt so good that I began to extend this attitude to my personal life as well with some very interesting results. My partner of many years is much younger than me and I always felt that I had to erase any age difference by being as fit as him, as hip as him and as career-orientated as him. What a joke that gets to be at forty, and a very cruel joke at that. So I began to wonder what I would be like on a personal level if I stopped all the obsessive exercise and competition and slowly with support I was able to do that. At the same time I got quite involved with the Friends (Quakers) and their calm non-verbal, non-ritualistic approach to spiritual life helped me a good deal with this. The discipline of just being quiet and present with myself, listening to what was going on inside my head and heart, was a new experience and this calm extended or combined with other emotional work I was doing in my life. I began writing again, at first a diary of my dreams and then short stories about people I had known.

The second part of my life is described more by interior challenges than exterior ones, and this has put me into a new relationship with men and women. The intensity of my relationship with my partner diminished which was good for both of us and I found space in my life for new friends and experiences. I find that younger people often want to be my friends and they tell me what they value in me . . . because I ask them. It's interesting to me what a man my age would have that would attract men and women in their twenties and thirties, and of course everyone loves to talk about themselves. They tell me that what they value is my life experience, my ability to see positive elements in being a gay man in a prejudiced society, and my sense of time. The last thing interests me because they say that I never rush anything and that when they are with me they feel that the time is completely theirs. I don't want to skirt the issue of sex as many of my younger friends would like to move our friendship into sexual activity as they say they find me attractive as well, but as a Christian in a long-term relationship I believe in and practise monogamy. That doesn't mean to say that I'm not tempted, but friendship, sharing and mutual support are much harder to come by than sex and why take the chance of giving up so much for so little?

It is not only younger people who find the qualities of mid-life attractive and appealing; mid-life men and women themselves report that when they have entered the second stage of life they have a new understanding of love and sexual expression. Confidence is a key word which keeps appearing in conversation with those who are well into their forties, and this confidence is reflected in how they speak of themselves and their lovers. This sense of confidence comes from half a lifetime of experience in developing relationships, and at mid-life we are often sure of what it is we want. The most common qualities described are patience, discretion, humour, understanding, maturity and often glamour. The intensity of love relationships which often characterizes the first stage of life is remembered with some sense of nostalgia but few would want to return to that phase, or even expect to. Relationships of long standing which have grown and matured into mid-life reflect the positive gifts mentioned above.

Doris and her husband, Eric, have been married for over twenty-five years and both are entering their fifties.

My love for Eric has changed greatly over the past ten years, and I can say that I probably love him more deeply since we entered mid-life than before. He seems to have more time for me and for our sex life as well now that he has stopped trying to set the world on fire. We also have more time for each other as the children have grown up, and we've looked towards ourselves and our relationship rather than outside to other people or new partners. We've been able to cast off some of our old habits which seemed to keep us apart and look for new ways of being together, physically and emotionally. I'm very glad we didn't give up on our marriage when things were difficult earlier on. Now, I appreciate Eric's sensitivity when it comes to sex and he takes time to please me and himself rather than rushing into bed and off to sleep after sex. We've found that bed is a good place for more than just sleep or sex, and some of our best conversations are before and after

130

sex. We went through a period in our forties where we both felt unattractive because our bodies were ageing, but that was part of the mid-life process. I would rather have the Eric I know than a young beautiful body without any miles on it. Rather than concentrating on how we look for sexual excitement, we focus on what we know pleases one another. I love to dress up and go out for dinner followed by a walk or a film. This usually is followed by a talk as we get ready for bed and then we are both in the mood for sex . . . or perhaps not. That's quite important to us, not to have sex if we aren't feeling like it. We always know there's another night because we're confident each other will be there in the morning.

Eric agrees with his wife but emphasizes different qualities of their mid-life romance and sex life. He appreciates the attention which Doris puts into dressing attractively when they go out.

I love being seen with a glamorous, well-dressed woman like Doris. I might lust after some of the younger women in a restaurant, but when I look at Doris I see the beauty that only the joyful and painful experiences of life can bring, and that's quite sexy. It's the difference between baked custard and creme caramel: one is quite smooth, bland and beautiful and the other is the same dish with an added complexity and surprise.

Both partners have learned to appreciate what they have earned through life experience and see that time brings a richness and complexity which is lacking in the young. By letting go of the images of their youthful selves, Eric and Doris have been able to look at who they are today and value their personal qualities in mid-life. Some aspects of their youth are to be mourned and released, and many mid-life men and women are more than eager and happy to give up some of the tensions and expectations carried around in the first stage of life. 'To be quite frank, I don't have to perform or be a sexual athlete for Doris. I know that I'm good enough for her and that our sex together is an expression of how we feel about the people we've become more than it is about what we can get up to. Sometimes it's quite good, sometimes it's adequate, but it's always more than just a quick release of sexual tension or energy'. Doris agrees, 'I think mid-life sex is about what's inside and underneath the façade; what I see in lots of young people is surface flash because they haven't had the time to develop inside. But then I guess that's what mid-life is all about . . . appreciating the people we've become.'

Appreciating the people we've become is also the key in accepting our potential for growth and an important step in mid-life is coming to terms with a physically ageing body. Previously we have discussed how some mid-life men and women struggle to maintain a physical appearance which belies their age. This is almost always a futile task and one which can become obsessive and eventually self-destructive. However, a reasonable approach to exercise can allow one to regain a sense of vigour and vitality which is one of the most useful tools in mid-life renegotiation. It is quite common for middle-aged people to stop any form of exercise other than the occasional Sunday walk and retreat into a sedentary life focusing around television, reading and eating too much. This retreat from the physicality of the first stage of life can be a subtle defence against the ageing process and is often used as an excuse for not taking on new challenges or realizing the potential of the second stage of life. Too many mid-lifers hide behind a layer of fat which shouts to the world, 'I am middle aged, I don't have to try any more, I am getting old'. It is a courageous move towards emotional health to shed the layers of fat and to discover the person that is hidden underneath.

A balanced approach to exercise is recommended by most doctors, but some will argue that exercise only increases one's sense of well being, rather than general health. Actually, this is the most important factor for mid-life men and women – an increased sense of well being – as at this time of our lives we often feel fatigued, mildly depressed and can experience bouts of free floating anxiety. Moderate exercise is the most immediate and convenient solution for many of the niggling little complaints we experience. Simple routines of stretching and flexibility exercises can loosen tight joints and muscles which are reluctant to get going in the morning. Walking vigorously is the best way to begin and an even better way to continue is to explore sports which one can do with a partner. Several studies have shown that a moderate exercise regime can be as effective as drugs when dealing with depression. Many men and women find that tennis, jogging or exercise classes give them an opportunity for rediscovering their partners in a different way as well as making them feel better physically. As well as being a priest, university chaplain and one of the authors of this book, Alvin is also a fitness instructor in the Fitness Centre at London Guildhall University.

> The Sports Organizer recruited me to teach introductory classes because she knew I ran and worked out, and she also knew how I felt about giving up on your body when you turn forty. She encouraged me to take an instructor's course and when the new Centre opened in the spring I started teaching. It's interesting to see the reactions of the young people when they see a fifty-year-old man lecturing them on the benefits of an exercise programme and then demonstrating equipment. It's probably even more surprising to see the university chaplain doing it, but lots of the students who come through the gym are mature men and women in their late thirties and forties, so I don't think I'm a bad role model. For me exercise has been a important ingredient in maintaining a positive self-image and dealing with my anxiety problems. I find that the physical release and confidence which comes from exercise ameliorates a lot of the small worries I have about life, my existential anxiety. Also, I feel better when I'm fit and the spin-offs are really worth the little time it takes to keep my weight down and my ageing muscles toned: I can wear the clothes I like rather than choosing for comfort or for camouflage quality; I have more energy to lead the busy life I have chosen in mid-life, and my physical confidence spills over into my emotional life as well.

> Simple exercise, like walking, can be a really effective management tool for mid-life, to use business language. My co-author, Shirley, suffers from chronic arthritis and some days when we work I can see the tension on her face from the pain. She's not the kind of person to give in easily, just the opposite actually, and I know that she walks to work from London Bridge almost everyday. That's a good thirty minutes if you move along briskly, and she says that it not only helps keep her joints flexible but also gives her time to think about her busy day and to put things in

perspective. In no way is Shirley an exercise freak, no step classes or hours on the stationary bicycle to tone her mid-life body, but she has integrated exercise into the idea of who she is in the second stage of her life. You can see the relaxed confidence keeping fit brings in her body language and in the way she wears her smart clothes.

Mid-life is an opportunity to rebalance one's life and to bring into equality the disparate aspects of our inner life and physical appearance. The two are closely linked and the growth in one will inevitably influence the other. It is a mistake to believe that the mid-life journey is solely about the inner life, and for educated cerebral people this is the great danger. It is all too easy to lose touch with our bodies and to feel that it is an arena in which only the young can play. It is also convenient to deny the life of the body as it is a simple way to ignore the fact that we are ageing. It is often too threatening to look at our bodies as they reflect dramatically how little time we have left and how much has gone before. The important element in taking hold of and accepting our changing self-image is to set realistic goals and models for ourselves in mid-life and to begin to love the adult we are becoming. Doris and Eric will never be the passionate lithe lovers of their youth, but they will be tender, considerate partners who know they are making love to someone who holds within them a world of shared experience. Sandra has emerged from the mountain of fat which protected her from the world of feeling and now lives a life renewed by negotiating a second stage of life based on her needs rather than the needs of others. Alvin will never win the London Marathon but he can feel comfortable and at home inside his fifty-plus body. By giving up the desperate fight to stave off change, Lionel has begun to live in the present and to hold hope for the future. Shirley will always live with physical discomfort but can feel a sense of control over it through her exercise and diet which give her the confidence to take on new challenges in mid-life. Paul can give up his punishing exercise programme and his anxiety about ageing to accept his gifts of maturity and judgement which bring him into closer relationship with people. These are men and women who have negotiated a peace with their bodies; they no longer see the ageing process as a war against time but rather as a co-operation with the inevitable process of being human. In their own ways they have come to love the middle-aged bodies they possess and to love the person it allows them to become.

8

WORK AND WORTH

Few elements of our lives define who we are as definitely as what we do for a living. Our work, and our success or failure there, is closely linked to how we perceive ourselves as people. In the first stage of life we make decisions about our careers which will define that sense of self-worth for many years, and many times these decisions are made to please our parents or our teachers as they are our guides and their role is to recognize and to encourage the gifts they see within us. However, our guides do not often listen to our voices but their own. You will remember from a previous chapter how one of the authors dreamed as a boy of being a foreign correspondent and how that dream stayed with him all his life as a romantic subtext until it resurfaced in mid-life in a new form. Only then could he begin to listen to his inner voice which had been ignored in the first stage of life. It is quite common for the dreams of adolescence to resurface during mid-life renegotiation, and it is also quite common to feel that they can be reclaimed in some manner. The mistake is to think that the dreams of the past need to be actualized in the present. They are rather the reminder and the call to a re-examination and to a deepening of our potential, rather than a map for the future. The mid-lifers who are able to tolerate the pain of lost dreams by holding them close as a reminder of who we might have been can use the lost past as a companion for planning a creative future.

The past, and the dreams of the past, whether they were our own or someone else's, can reveal a good deal to us about our relationship with work and achievement. On a return visit to his boyhood home in New Zealand an Anglican priest who is approaching forty spent a day sorting out the momentos from his adolescence. As a young man Mark competed in athletics with hopes of becoming a member of the New Zealand Olympic team and competing in the Commonwealth Games. Rated as a top junior sprinter while in secondary school and university, he suddenly quit at twenty supposedly to concentrate on his studies. Ironically, he only was allowed to attend university by his family if he chose to train for the law, a career which held no interest for him. After completing his degree he just as suddenly left New Zealand and became one of the band of Australasian wanderers which still fill London today. Ten years later, after a series of false starts in business careers, he realized a boyhood dream and offered himself for training as a priest in the Church of England. Now as he approached forty, Mark sorted the trophies of his adolescent achievements and reflected on the past.

> My mother had saved all the junk from my days as a runner – news clippings, trophies and even an enlarged photograph of me made into a poster. I'm breaking the tape at a junior meeting when I was nineteen just ahead of a guy I was always trying to beat; my long hair is blown out behind me and I have a look of concentration on my face that only the dedicated, or the driven, can achieve. I don't recognize that person at all, and I don't remember being that person at all. I quit competing a year later. Ten years later I thought I was in touch with that boy when I finally got the courage to train to be a priest. I felt I had this calling which no one had listened to and that the voice inside was saying that I was called by God. Now as I approach forty I realize that the dream was real as was the voice calling me, but that I didn't listen to what was being said. My inner voice, and I've begun to realize that we all have one, was calling me to serve others by serving myself first. At that time this was too radical for me to accept. I was the golden boy of my mother's life and my achievements on the athletic field were a redemption of her lost dreams. I was clever enough to know that at twenty but not quite clever enough at thirty to avoid exchanging one version of being a good boy for another. I don't regret training to be a priest, but I now realize that it was just the first step towards answering my inner voice to serve others. Today I work in the mental health

sector of the NHS, as a priest and as a psychotherapist, and the combination is quite important to me. I was never cut out to be a simple parish priest, the acceptable fantasy fed to me by the Anglo-Catholic priests of my childhood. I know now that I am neither a simple person nor a simple parish priest, but I am an excellent therapist, counsellor, pastor, teacher and group facilitator. Even at forty I struggle with fulfilling somebody else's idea of what I should be. Pleasing myself and realizing that this at the same time pleases God is a difficult concept to take on board, but I'm working on it.

I started my psychotherapy training ten years ago and since that time I've piled up one qualification after another and currently I am completing a masters degree. Recently a friend who was disappointed and angry because I was not willing to go on holiday with him because of work on my dissertation said to me, 'When you finish this MA you still won't be good enough you know. No matter how many pieces of paper you stick in your desk drawer you'll still be the little boy trying to please Mum and Dad. You're still running, Mark, and something inside you keeps moving the finish tape . . . you'll never finish the race and in the meantime I'll be getting a suntan in Greece!' I realize that I'm just beginning to come to terms with some kind of mid-life change and I'm feeling quite positive about it . . . it's a bit frightening, but I keep that poster of myself crossing the finish line in my study now, and when I look at that boy with his long hair straining to cross the finish line first, I try to tell myself that being first won't accomplish much because they'll always be another race and always be somebody just behind you to crowd you out of first place. Maybe I can stop running now.

Mark's story highlights the scenario which begins many mid-life renegotiations for both men and women. The theme of inner growth is most prevalent for men as that is often the very thing which they have avoided in the first stage of life. For Mark his longing to help others, first as a priest and now as a psychotherapist, can be seen as an expression of his own inner desire for a close, intimate relationship, one in which he can both care and be cared for. Peter O'Connor develops this idea in his excellent short book which focuses on the male mid-life renegotiation, *Understanding the Mid-Life Crisis*. We often reach the top rung of our career with a sense of emptiness and without the ability to feel fulfilled by our achievements. It is quite common at mid-life to examine what we have accomplished and the sacrifices we have made to get there and to find within us some feeling of resentment and ennui. Does the future just mean more of the same and where will the new challenges come from? For Mark it is within the sphere of self-realization and the journey for him is an inner one as he has come to realize that the outer journey is only half of the story. Many people arrive at this juncture in their lives due to an outside catalyst. In today's economic climate redundancy and the failure to achieve promotion are common experiences for mid-life men. It is at this time that men are able to come in touch with the disparity between their dreams and reality. It can be a particularly bitter experience if the dream was not one of their own making. For most men their occupation is closely tied up with their self-perception and questions about their worklife are in reality questions about themselves – who they are as people.

This call from the inner life is often a new experience for most men and it is not possible to over-emphasize its importance. The type of work in which one is involved can be the key to the examination process. At this point in life many men begin for the first time to understand the difference between work as a job and work as a vocation. They are able to acknowledge how closely their lives have been involved with power and money and how little with relationships and people. The information is not necessarily new but at mid-life we are often able to reorganize what we already know in a different manner. The bleeding heart liberal who has devoted his life to social work or medicine is suddenly seen as not a bad role model for the insurance executive. The lure here is that many men find a sense of emptiness in mid-life, especially if their careers have been about objects, facts and figures rather than people. However, it must be said that men in the helping professions do experience a similar examination process. They do not envy their business-orientated counterparts but can be plagued with a type of hopelessness which is unique to those who spend their work lives working for the good of others.

Their journeys are about valuing themselves and their own needs for these men have often given away all their 'selfish' desires out of guilt or the desire for closer ties with human relationships. Theirs will be an intensely personal journey towards accepting the validity of their own needs and desires. In mid-life men and women must come to a new understanding of their relationship to job and vocation. For most of us there will be a loosening of the ties with previous career identification and a move towards 'selfish' fulfilment. This is an important concept as in the first stage of life it is common to project our good qualities into work, institutions and other people. In short, we give away for a time all that we feel is worthy and valuable in us and place it in our careers. This often produces high achieving men and women who are noted for their dedication to their work and for their ability to create dynamically. Many women put these good qualities into building a family life and raising children and society honours this role; however, as children grow and leave home these women often find that they are left with little for themselves. If we give away so much of ourselves to our careers and to others, there must be an acknowledgement of that loss, and this comes at mid-life. It is the natural time for us to return to the 'selfish' position without being selfish.

In Christian communities it is not always the done thing to concentrate on personal development. The model of Jesus who gives his very existence for humankind is held up as a goal, but this twisting of the New Testament theology can result in a need-less feeling of being cheated because we always live for others. The model which Jesus provides for us is one of full development of our human potential for relationship which must come before we have something to give to others. The angry, empty, depressed man or woman of forty who resents the demands made of him or her by Church, society and family is hardly capable of achieving the model offered by most church communities. A re-examination of the ministry of Jesus will lead us to an understanding that we must fill ourselves first before we have gifts to give others. And this filling, or 'selfish', development is not about education, accomplishment, or material goods but rather about the inner life of feelings, the building of reciprocal relationships; in short, to care and to be cared for. For women this discovery of self can lead them back into the work-place where they often begin new and dynamic careers, and this will be discussed later in this chapter.

Many men only come into touch with their feelings of emptiness about their careers through their dreams where their anger is expressed to them. Jon told his counsellor this dream.

> I am in a locked room and there seems to be no way out, but I have a tremendous sense that I must escape. The impossibility of escape is overwhelming and I begin to beat at the walls of this steel room and a door opens and I move into another room. The room is full of plants and soft furnishings but as I begin to relax I see that behind the plants are walls of steel. I am trapped again only this time it's not an unpleasant prison – but it's still a prison. I start beating the walls, knocking over the plants and upsetting the furniture. A door opens in the wall and I go into yet another room and my father is waiting there for me, reaching out with his hand. I move towards him but he disappears and the steel walls of this room begin to close in on me. I will be smashed unless I can break out of this room but I can't hit the walls because they are closing in on me. I will die. Just before the walls pressed in on me I awoke and found myself standing beside the bed stamping my foot and shouting, 'No, No, No!'

Jon's terrifying dream was related to his frustration at work and the sense of betrayal which he was feeling at not being valued for the work he was doing. As a middle manager at forty-five he was realizing that the promotions were coming more slowly now and that he was faced with a work-life which would be described by repetition of what had gone before. His bosses had decided that Jon had reached the zenith of his creative abilities and that younger men possessed the vision to move his department forward. Of course Jon did not share this view and was trapped by his anger with no way forward. For someone like Jon the growth path is not looking forward to more accomplishment and power but rather looking to the side. He was presented with an opportunity to look at what he had left behind in his path to success and perhaps to reclaim some of it as working tools for a renewed midlife.

141

At mid-life it is important to place the lure of money and power in its proper perspective. In our capitalist production-driven society these are the two key elements in most men's lives regardless of what career they choose. Even those in the helping professions are swept up by pay gradings, promotions which can be disguised as merely opportunities to help more people and to influence policy, and the desire to replace bad management with their own enlightened version of power. It is almost impossible to escape the desire for power and money as in our world it validates to society who we are. We must be important or worthy men and women if we are in a senior position or earn a high salary. The other danger at mid-life is to take a high-minded attitude towards this dynamic duo – money and power – and to reject them as unimportant elements in our lives. At mid-life we are given yet another opportunity to put money and power into perspective in our lives and to recognize their allure as well as the benefits they bring. Jon felt trapped in a steel room by his job, a prisoner of his own success without opportunities for change or growth. His immediate reaction was a desire to break out and to leave his job to retrain in a more caring or more 'enlightened' profession.

Through his work with his therapist he came to see the importance of his father in the dream and the message of the beckoning hand. Jon's father had died two years prior to the dream and they had not been particularly close. Jon had finished university, unlike his father, and had risen quickly in the banking world. Jon's mother was very proud of his success and the security he had achieved as his father had drifted from job to job which paid barely enough to support the family. Jon described his father as a happy man who loved playing music in pubs after work; besides bringing in extra money he obviously loved the camaraderie of pub life and the friends he made around his native County Clare. At his funeral over five hundred people turned up and the wake went on until well past midnight with food, music and lots of drinking. 'In some way it was a real tribute to the man by all those people who loved him. I will always regret that I couldn't bring myself to attend. My mother and I sat at home watching television that night as we sorted out my father's clothes.' Jon's dream became the key element in his mid-life renegotiation and he returned to it time and again for reinterpretation and support. One possible interpretation of Jon's dream is that his father was beckoning him towards the inner life which could release him from his anger and despair. Jon was being invited not forward but to the side by his father. While not being an appropriate guide for the first stage of his life, Jon's father, even in his death, became a harbinger of what could be.

Jon was able to make use of his dream to release his angry feelings and to accept his accomplishments and success without wanting more of the same. He decided that his bosses might well be correct in their evaluation of him, and that there were other avenues for him to go down. For Jon the growth was not in abandoning his job for some glamorous alternative but a continuance of satisfaction in his work combined with a new ability to enjoy life in a more relaxed manner. It would be convenient to say that Jon started playing the fiddle in North London pubs but that was not the case as that would have been inappropriate for him. As he began to accept with new confidence his work situation, he found time for other challenges in his outside life through work in his church and his love for walking and painting. The father of Jon's dream was not saying to him, 'Be like me', but rather, 'Come along with me and see what beauty can be found in other human beings'. The goal in mid-life is not to cast off or to reject the past as this is the very content of who we have become. At mid-life we are given an opportunity, like Jon, to reorganize what we have built in the first stage of life and to plan consciously a new life of our own for the future.

In mid-life women often find that their journey will take them back to the work-place in new and creative ways. It is a fact that more and more women are entering the workforce since the end of the Second World War; some figures show that the percentage has increased to over 60 per cent of married women. This has implications for men as well as women because women bring different priorities to their careers. In mid-life men may be looking inward to uncover what can be seen as the feminine side of their natures, that part of them which looks to building relationships with people, sharing their feelings, and working in co-operation, but many women are setting different agendas for themselves. This is not to say that women who go back to work in mid-life become aggressive over-achievers like many of their male counterparts, although this can be a temptation. What does happen though is that mid-life women who have spent many years building and maintaining family relationships are now seeking to move in a wider world, and that world is often found in the work-place. The majority of mature students at the 'new universities' in Britain are mid-life women who are studying for careers in a wide variety of fields. Marianne is typical of many mid-life women as she returned to work full-time after her divorce.

Sometimes I think my life is a cliché. I was happily and obliviously married for twenty years with a successful husband and two beautiful sons. One day my husband came home and said he was in love with a younger woman, that she was pregnant and that he was moving in with her. My safe middle-class world disappeared overnight and was replaced with loneliness, anger and despair. For a few months I became someone I didn't like very much: bitter and vindictive without any hope for the future. What's a forty-five-year-old woman to do? My sons were great but they were caught between supporting me and not wanting to lose the father they loved. I soon saw that my anger and bitterness were preventing them from maintaining what I had tried to build for twenty years, so I tried to work through my feelings. Luckily the curate in our parish was a trained counsellor and I spent a good deal of time with him just unloading my frustrations. But I couldn't get over the sense that my life contained no possibilities for growth or happiness; I see now that I was still defining myself by who I had been, not by who I could be. I was willing to admit my loss and to grieve for it, but I wasn't quite ready to start living a new life.

I got involved in church activities which was a good way of filling my time and eventually I began to translate the courage and strength I found in Scripture into my own life. I often felt like poor old Job heaping ashes on myself as I sat in a dung heap, if you can call a smart four-bedroom house in Sydenham a dung heap. Like in most grieving processes, time was a great healer and through exploring my spiritual life I began to understand what forgiveness and reconciliation meant. I began to disengage emotionally from my ex-husband and to see myself as Marianne, the person, not Marianne, the wife of somebody. Like many women in my position, I did not have enough to live on and I was determined not to take money from my ex-husband so I had to find a way to support myself. I had done an art therapy diploma course and worked casually for many years while the children were growing up, but I didn't feel qualified for full-time work. However, I had no choice. What I ended up with were three part-time jobs which gave me enough to live on but required me to rush from one end of London to another several times a week. The surprising thing was that I really began to enjoy it after being housebound for so many years. Each week I felt more and more competent as I would arrive at my three little jobs, and when the pay cheques began arriving I started to believe that I would make it after all. But the most important thing was not the money; it was a growing sense of myself as a valuable and respected person that was the surprising spin-off from the work. I found out so many things about myself and I guess that is one of the interesting things about mid-life, finding the person you are under all that stuff which has gone before. I found out that I could make friends easily, that I had a sense of humour, that I was very good at my job, and that people wanted to make use of my professional skills. Eventually as a lark, I did an evening management training course at what was then our local polytechnic and now I'm managing a team of specialist therapists for one of the new health care trusts.

It may sound dramatic but my mid-life journey had put me in touch with my power as a woman and as a human being. My faith and the love and support of my sons played a big role in my renewed life. I've also learned not to repeat the mistakes of the past and how to say 'No'. A year ago a man I was dating asked me to marry him and offered a life of security which was similar to what I had with my ex-husband. I liked the man and I may even have loved him, but I was not willing to give up all that I had worked for over the past five years for a comfortable

145

retirement and companionship. I've got too many things I want to do before I settle down again.

Marianne's mid-life renegotiation contains many aspects which will be a familiar story to mid-life women. The challenge presented by the unavoidable crisis of her divorce thrust her into a world she had been separated from for most of her life. While most women do not deny their potential for careers they often put them aside to concentrate on traditional female roles, and the uncovering of the creative energies inside can be part of a great rediscovery process.

This rediscovery of personal strength is not without its problems as many women face difficult adjustments in the working world. Women are often a threat to men in the work-place and mid-life women returning to new work can be resented by their male colleagues and accused of losing their femininity. However, when women talk about their experience in the work-place they rarely reveal any sense of this. In fact, they usually report an increased desire to dress smartly and in a feminine manner, and it is usually the mid-life women in offices who set the standards. One health care manager says, 'I never have to tell my older staff that they need to smarten up their appearance; it's always the younger women who dress too casually or want to wear trousers and baggy jumpers. My older women staff seem to be much more confident that it's alright to be seen as womanly and attractive'.

The threat to men when they find women as their supervisors or colleagues is even more apparent in relationships where both partners have challenging careers. Sam and Anna came to counselling because they felt that their commitment to their jobs was destroying the intimacy of their relationship. Sam had worked for many years as a chartered accountant and when they were in their late thirties Anna returned to teaching and was soon made a deputy headteacher. Sam expressed feelings of being no longer important to Anna and indicated her commitment to work as the basis for the problems in the marriage. His job was demanding and he suspected that Anna wanted him to work less and take more responsibility for managing their home life. For her part, Anna felt that Sam was jealous of her success in an exciting world while he was trapped behind a desk adding up boring columns of figures. She asserted that for many years she sat at home while Sam was out in the world making things happen and that now it was her turn to exercise her creative powers. The couple wanted to remain together but could not see a way through the impasse of their conflicting jobs and the apparent jealously held by both parties. As in many mid-life scenarios Sam and Anna were at a stage in their lives where they were beginning to re-evaluate what had gone before. In some ways, Anna was further along in the process than Sam as she understood that she was pursuing a new life path which spoke to her needs in the second stage of life. However, Anna complained of always feeling guilty about liking her job and for the time she spent at school. She felt that Sam was asking her to give up her newfound competence and freedom in order to save the marriage.

For Sam, the counselling gave him an opportunity to look at his male-oriented attitude of locating his inner needs and inner life in the external world of work. Sam's mid-life renegotiation came at a time when he was experiencing a serious dissatisfaction at the disparity between his youthful dreams of success and the reality of his achievements. Anna's new and successful career only heightened and intensified his feelings that he was being abandoned when he needed her the most. He also came to understand that his finding fault in their relationship was in some way a reflection of his inability to find faults in himself and to deny his needs for intimacy and his inability to express his feelings. As his skills at inward reflection increased Sam became less and less threatened by Anna's commitment to her job, and he slowly took a fair share of responsibility for the emotional health of their relationship. This change in their marriage gave Anna the opportunity for the first time to enjoy her success.

Mid-life women do not seem to experience the same dissatisfaction with success in their careers as do their male counterparts. While this may well be due to the fact that they often enter careers at a later stage or return to old ones given up at an earlier time, they often are able to accept their accomplishments and to balance them against other parts of their lives. Men are told from a very early age that they will be expected to have a career in the outside world and that it should be a successful one. Peter O'Connor says, 'These are the goals that a male is given in adolescence, and in this sense a man's emotional development can be seen as being fixated at this stage, with no direction, goals or guide-lines for life beyond adolescence. Men are in no way prepared for the possibility of achieving success and all its paraphernalia. Hence they are left with a pervasive feeling that it is all a massive hoax and that success is a totally vacuous notion. Such a perception contributed greatly to ... feeling[s] of betrayal, depression and futility'. If O'Connor is to be believed, then Sam's feelings are understandable, and one is able to see why Anna found it difficult to take her success seriously.

While women may feel a desire to return to work or to prepare for an exciting new career as their children leave home, men often have strong urges to do just the opposite. Mid-life men almost universally present to their counsellors a deep dissatisfaction with their current job or occupation which often manifests itself as boredom, frustration and depression. It is not uncommon for these men to experience serious health problems which facilitate a mid-life career change. At mid-life the sense that time is running out is around for everyone over the age of forty and a panic is heightened by the financial and family responsibility that most middle-aged men carry. Julian came to counselling at forty-two because he was frightened: frightened about the urges he was feeling and frightened by the idea that he might act on them. A tall, slender, handsome man who was a successful sales executive for a computer software corporation, he hesitantly explained his feelings without any expression of emotion.

> I'm forty-two and I have the best job in my area. I also earn lots of money which makes me pleased and certainly maintains my family well. My wife is a nice person and a good mother to our three children. All my friends and family think I'm the perfect son, father and businessman. I have every reason in the world to be happy. I don't know if I should really be here or not, but every morning I wake up after only a couple of hours' sleep and get ready for work. The family is usually gone by then. The last few months I just can't get going and I sit in the garden drinking

148

coffee, smoking and staring off into space. I don't know what I'm feeling but I do know that I don't want to go to work. At the last possible minute, I get in the car and I'm overcome by a desire to just keep on driving . . . anywhere but to work. I want to drive out of this life to somewhere else. I just want to be something different, a different life . . . something more. I couldn't do it of course because I love my family and my wife. The only reason I'm here with you is that I'm afraid that some morning I will just keep on driving. Now that they have finished the Channel Tunnel I could imagine myself just driving straight through to France and maybe things would change . . . maybe it would be magic.

Julian's powerful fantasy is not that atypical of mid-life men and contains the beginning themes of his mid-life renegotiation. His fears were identified as his grief at the passing of time, his youth, his family growing up and getting ready to leave, and the surety that his youthful dreams had passed. We usually associate grief and loss with physical death, but in mid-life there is a good deal of grieving and mourning for both men and women to complete before moving into the second stage of life. One of the problems with this type of grief is that it is not socially acceptable; certainly Julian's family and colleagues would have assumed he was having a nervous breakdown, and the authors feel that many of the so-called 'nervous breakdowns' diagnosed in the past by professionals were in fact cases of mid-life grief. Julian could not identify what it was that was lost and was frightened by not having any reason to feel sad. As Julian allowed himself to talk he was able to identify to some degree his fear of the future and loss of youthful ambition and drive. He didn't want to be young again, but he wasn't ready to give up the sense that life still held meaning and challenge.

'I feel like I'm frozen in a block of ice, waiting for someone to set me free. My wife says that I don't listen to her, but what she doesn't understand is that I can't hear her. I feel trapped and that's why I just want to keep on driving until I reach some place warm . . . then perhaps I'll unfreeze.' Julian's ice images and his desire for someone or something external to set him free are also indicative of the closing down of his emotional potential for creative growth. He slowly began to thaw as he shared his daydreams and fantasies which centred around his desire to be in closer relationship with people, to do something creative, and to slow down advancing time. Julian often spoke about wanting to paint in the South of France even though he said he had no artistic talent or experience. By allowing himself to entertain these fantasies he began to break his inertia and give up the idea that he was too old or too embedded in his present life to make any changes.

Eventually he began to share his fantasies with his wife and family who were surprisingly supportive of his 'dropping out' scenario. Julian reported,

> When I told her about wanting to go to France to paint she laughed and said, 'OK, let's do it. We'll sell the house, cash in the insurance, and go. The boys can grow potatoes to feed us and we'll keep chickens in the kitchen'. I haven't laughed so much in months, and we opened a second bottle of wine to celebrate the move. Of course we aren't going to do it, though when we teased the boys about it they thought it was a great idea, but we were celebrating our laughter and the sharing. I felt like the ice cube was beginning to drip a bit at the edges.

Changes like the one in Julian's fantasy are usually too drastic for mid-life men and women to contemplate and are not advisable. This kind of change presents a much too abrupt a transition for most personalities to experience, but entertaining the fantasy is an important step in learning to listen to our inner voice. The voice which tells us that we need to change is an important guide and is not to be ignored out of fear that we might act upon it. Sometimes these fantasies take the form of wanting to make a dramatic career switch, say from accountancy to landscape gardening, but again if we listen closely we can discern that the call is to a more authentic version of whom we might be. Allowing ourselves to play with the possibilities is a healthy method of confronting the move into mid-life and Julian's family accompanied him on his journey, both emotionally and physically.

We took a month's holiday without any previous planning. Susan and I put the boys in the car and we started driving, to France strangely enough. We didn't know where we were going but we got there, found a place to stay, and 'dropped out' for a whole month. It was wonderful to just let the days take their own form and we spent surprisingly little money. We found a flat in Bordeaux for a week and then the landlady told us about a house in the country where we ended up spending the rest of the time. There were no chickens in the kitchen, but on the ferry on the way back I realized I was happy. Somehow the month in France with the people I love the most gave me some sense that there was still hope for me. I don't know quite yet where it will all end up, but I'm thinking about what I might do with the skills I have rather than trying to acquire new ones. I've always wanted to be my own boss, so that's a possibility because I know an awful lot about computer software. We'll have to wait and see.

Julian was just at the beginning of what was to be a successful mid-life renegotiation because he was able to access his inner voice, the bit inside of us all which speaks of the authentic self.

For some the inner voice will lead them along new paths and one of the most common for many Christian men and women is a call to full-time ministry experienced in mid-life. A surprising number of people offer themselves for ministry at this time of their lives, and this decision needs to be examined closely by both the individuals and the Church before proceeding. This desire can represent many things for the mid-life man or woman and it is useful to examine some of the possible motivations. Such a decision is always the expression of a desire for a deeper spiritual life and a closer relationship with God. However, those who are ordained ministers report that one of the most difficult aspects of full-time ministry is that one is so caught up with other people's spiritual lives and the day-to-day administration of parish life that there is little time for personal prayer and meditation. It is easy to romanticize the life of parish clergy and the reality is almost always more mundane than supposed. The effects on established family life are at the least stressful and at the worst disastrous, and more clergy marriages end than is commonly supposed. Partners find the new role of clergy spouse comes with both written and unwritten expectations which they may not have bargained for. The recent popularity of Joanna Trollope's *The Rector's Wife* gives a view of the tensions in a clergy marriage when the ordained partner focuses his energy on his career and the needs of other people. There is little room for the needs of the family and the parish claims a large part of the emotional resources previously given to the spouse and family. Men and women who report a sudden conversion experience in mid-life are often drawn to full-time ministry as they tie this experience closely to their rebirth or movement into the second stage of life. It is as if they used a tool to solve a difficult problem and in gratitude want to make that tool their own; in secular life it is common for mid-lifers to form deep and painful transference attachments to their therapists and often want to train as counsellors. While the importance of a rediscovered or new spiritual life is an event to be honoured, it need not lead to professional ministry, and those who feel the call to train must examine their motivations closely.

Perhaps the most difficult and most unsettling scenario for everyone involved is when a mid-lifer feels called directly by God to take up full-time ministry, and the best possible advice for these situations is to take every step very slowly. Evelyn, a fifty-year-old woman, came to the chaplain at the university where she worked as telephonist to announce that she was hearing messages from God. The chaplain knew her as a volunteer in the chapel where she played the organ for services. She related how she had returned to the Church after her children had left home and how important it had become for her. Evelyn was active in her local parish church and her husband reluctantly went along on Sundays as well. For the past several months when she played the organ in the university chapel she felt she was hearing messages from God which indicated that he wanted her to become a priest. 'While I'm playing I hear a voice saying, "Come to me", or "Serve me".' This she interpreted as a call from God and a command to give up her job at the university and present herself for training. While it is easy to dismiss Evelyn's experience as the onset of menopause or mid-life *angst*, it is important to give respect to her spiritual life. It is always a good idea to be suspicious of people who feel that they have a direct line to God which is quite different from describing one's spiritual dialogue with God as a personal relationship as this direct line relationship can be used to support behaviour one would not otherwise undertake. However, sudden conversion combined with a new and close relationship with God, should flash red lights to the listener or at least yellow, proceed slowly, lights. But there are positive moves into full-time ministry in mid-life as well, and these are usually undertaken by men and women who have a long relationship with the Church and their own spiritual life. One of the authors of this book speaks of his move from teaching to ministry when he was in his early forties.

> I never wanted to leave teaching because it was my vocation, and my work with adolescents had been one of the centres of my life for almost fifteen years. I was raised in the Church and as a teenager considered becoming a minister while I was preparing for university. However, other things got in the way, like my social life, like the Vietnam War, like political commitments. For many years I stayed away from church life and was quite cynical about the hypocrisy of clergy and Christian people in general. After my daughter was born I returned and became quite involved in my local parish where I was on the PCC and taught in the Sunday School programme. As I approached forty I began to question what I was doing with my life and what kind of challenge I wanted for the second half. I never seriously considered training for ministry as it sounded frighteningly disruptive to my comfortable California lifestyle, not to mention how socially unacceptable it would be to my friends. However, I did become more and more involved in church activities and my spiritual life was renewed and deepened by this participation and by the guidance of my parish priest. Part of my mid-life renegotiation was clearly tied up with my commitment to the Christian faith, so I did not completely reject the idea that I might have something to offer the Church while still remaining in my teaching job. After several years I was encouraged to train as a Permanent Deacon in the American Episcopal Church which is a non-stipendiary

ordained position. I was accepted for training after a year's waiting and another six months of interviews and evaluations. From
the first day at the School for Deacons in San Francisco I knew I
was in the wrong place but was too frightened at what that might
mean. I guess my story is one of long resistance to the inevitable
and eventually I just gave up and talked with my Bishop. As they
say, the rest is history, but a history filled with a lot of changes,
many of which have been very painful. Fortunately, I never had
any fantasies about the wonderful life enjoyed by Christian ministers; I had known too many clergy too intimately to delude
myself on that score. Looking back from the perspective of ten
years I now can see how the decision was inevitable and how
integral it was in my mid-life change; however, I'm glad I didn't
rush it. One of the good things we learn in mid-life is that though
time is slipping away there is no need to get things done immediately. In areas like this God has his own time frame and it is best
to wait and to discern how God is speaking to you . . . not directly
necessarily but through the people and events in your life and
then to apply your own gifts of reason to the decision and to
balance that decision against the wisdom and tradition of the
Church. That sounds very Anglican, doesn't it?

This chapter opened with a discussion of the importance of
work in our lives and how our careers define our sense of self in
the first stage of life. At mid-life it is appropriate to re-examine
our philosophy of work and worth and to determine what an
appropriate model would be for the second stage of life. As our
career choices are usually defined by others, no matter how well
meaning they may have been, some readjustment is often appropriate in mid-life. This does not always mean a dramatic change
in direction; in fact it can mean a reaffirmation of earlier decisions.
It is important to understand whether one's job is an occupation
or vocation and whether the fulfilment comes intrinsically from
the work or from the feeling of power that being productive and
in control can bring. The sense of being trapped which many mid-
life men and women experience often proceeds from doing work
which no longer meets their emotional needs as they move into
mid-life. As mid-life is often a time when relationships become

more important than material success, many mid-lifers will begin
to look for ways to develop opportunities for this work. However,
the important factor in developing a reordered philosophy of
work and worth is listening to the inner voice spoken of earlier in
this chapter. Perhaps it would be useful to clarify that the concept
of the inner voice is merely a poetic way of speaking about what
we know is true inside us. The New Zealand priest, Mark, took
twenty years to access his inner voice after many false starts and
found it was saying to him that he wanted to care and to be cared
for. This has lead him into a successful and fulfilling journey
towards an adjustment of his original career decisions. Jon's inner
voice revealed to him the emptiness of his drive for money and
power, and as he listened he gave up his need for control replac-
ing it with deeper and more relaxed relationships with people.
Marianne's inner voice led her to a discovery of her own personal
strength and assisted her in rebuilding a shattered life. Alvin
fought his inner voice for many years, and while giving in to what
he knew was right brought many painful changes, he now sees
his life as fulfilled in a way he never experienced in the first stage
of life. And perhaps most poignant of all, Julian's inner voice lead
him to thaw the iceberg inside his soul and to begin living again.

9

CHANGING FACES

I live my life in growing orbits
which move out over the things of the world.
Perhaps I can never achieve the last,
but that will be my attempt.
I am circling around God, around the ancient tower,
and I have been circling for a thousand years,
and I still don't know if I am falcon, or storm,
or a great song.

This excerpt from a poem by the German poet, Rilke, has been following one of the authors around for over a quarter of a century. Like an old friend which one loses contact with and who then suddenly turns up in an unexpected context, the poem with its images of an ever present journey towards the mind of God is an appropriate opening to this chapter which will discuss the changed person we may well become in mid-life. This book has been about facing changes and the development of an authentic identity drawn from inner resources for the second stage of life. When this is begun we will never see the same face in the mirror again; the wrinkles, the crows feet, the map of our lives which is written on our skin will always be a part of us, but a new face will slowly begin to emerge.

If the reader takes nothing else away from this book than the idea that mid-life is both a spiritual and an emotional journey, then the authors will feel that they have accomplished their task. In the widest sense of the concept, our brief lives are about a dialogue with God, and the poet's image of a falcon circling the ancient tower is both beautiful and useful: as we come closer to

God on our flight, we are renewed by this closeness and in a sense reborn as a new person. There is no magic here; we are still the same person. We look the same, our lives do not always change dramatically and our history is still our own. The past remains with us, but in mid-life its power to control can be loosened. What is needed for most people is a time out at mid-life, a pause on life's journey; it is essential consciously to experience mid-life for growth to occur. It does not happen naturally. What does happen naturally is a suggestion to examine our lives at this time. It may be a call from our inner voice, a dramatic life change due to illness, the death of someone close or our parents, or a profound experience of depression or hopelessness. Regardless of the form, it is imperative that we stop and listen.

There are only two stories to tell in this short chapter, but they are stories which embody the possibility for growth and change in mid-life. One of the stories is about courage, pain, loss and new growth; the other is about pain and loss as well but centres around someone who has failed to grasp the essential elements of mid-life renegotiation. One of the people is still circling the ancient tower which Rilke uses to represent God, but she is caught up in a storm of self-doubt and self-obsession which holds her away from growth. The other person is now dead, but as he approached mid-life he grasped the challenge with courage and became the falcon in the poem. Both of the stories are about approaching the great song of life; one of the people heard the music and danced to it, the other is still caught in her storm and perhaps the music will yet be heard through the thunder and lightning.

Sophie has experienced great pain and loss in her life from an early age. As an only child of emotionally distant parents she began her journey without the knowledge that she could be loved as the person she is. Her early years were a series of attempts to engage her parents in an emotional dialogue which only resulted in disappointment, and she became even more alienated from the world of feelings. She married in a further attempt to establish emotional bonding with another person, but after ten years she and her husband separated. She told her husband, 'I thought I loved you but I don't know what love is. Sometimes I like you, but I feel that you are trying to possess me with all your attention and care. I need time by myself to find who I am and what I want'. At forty Sophie found herself alone with a good job, a secure financial life, and the respect of her professional colleagues, but without any close relationships. At this time she entered therapy with a psychiatrist and ten years later is still attending weekly sessions with him. While this therapeutic relationship has formed a secure core for her life, she has not been able to move beyond it. Over the years Sophie has ventured into a myriad of alternative therapies searching for the key which will unlock her cold emotional world, but she has never been able to stick with any one long enough to learn if it would be the right one for her.

Initially she tried religion and joined a congregation of supportive and caring Christians, but within a year she began to feel that she couldn't believe in the same way as they did. Eventually she drifted away and part of the ending process for her was the need to reject organized religion as hypocritical. What she criticized about the church members seemed to be their very humanity. Their inability to be perfect models of Christian charity and love were, ironically, the very aspects of her personality which she loathed. What followed was a journey through new age therapies, dieticians prescribing cleansing foods and purifying regimens, women's support groups which encouraged her to access her anger towards men, a variety of hobbies which were quickly abandoned, and exercise classes which promised a new body and peace of mind. Along the way she collected a stack of self-help manuals ranging from those which advocated getting in touch with the child inside to others which encouraged her to recall abusive elements in her childhood. At fifty, Sophie feels even more lonely and alienated than when she began her mid-life journey, and the one element which has remained constant in her search for fulfilment is her therapeutic relationship. Her emotional life is still described by self-obsessive examination and a narcissistic tendency which prevents her from moving outside her own world of pain and victimization. From the authors' point of view, Sophie was given the opportunity to stop and listen to her inner voice which spoke to her about the emptiness which she experienced at the core of her life. What she has not been able to do is to move courageously outside that pain to make contact with other human beings, as the second stage of life is about human relationships rather than solely about one's own self. The storm continues for Sophie and she is caught up in the roar of the thunder which prevents her from hearing not only her own inner voice but the voices of others calling out to her. Sophie continues to be blinded by the lightning of the storm and is unable to recognize relationships of quality when they are presented to her as her suspicion of others' motives is omnipresent.

The second story comes from the authors' many years of involvement in HIV/AIDS and is about one of the first men to die of AIDS-related illness in England. Initially, John's story is no less dark and it begins well within his own personal storm of pain and loss. John was raised in a family where he was the centre of attention, and his early years were filled with his mother's attempts to deal with her own depression by showering love and attention on her son. He learned at an early age that to be loved he had to perform, to fulfil others in some way that would get their attention. He never successfully separated from his mother who would alternate her obsessive attention towards him with arbitrary times of indifference. Needless to say, this left John with a very skewed view of love and his ability to obtain it. As a gay man he realized that he needed to leave his small town if he was to live a free and independent life. In the London of the 1970s John found himself drawn into a cosmopolitan lifestyle which never resulted in any long-term relationships. For ten years his life centred around going to the gym to perfect the body which would make him desirable in his social world and developing his professional life as a graphic designer which gave him the money to live independently and lavishly. 'I was convinced that if I was beautiful and rich I would find someone to love me. What I found was that there were lots of people who would desire me, but none who would love me . . . or none I would allow to love me.'

In his late thirties John contracted hepatitis B and was hospitalized for two months and this event became the creative illness which began the changes in his life. Lying in the hospital bed John was forced to rely on his own inner resources as his casual friends soon stopped visiting. He used this time to examine his life and wonder where he was going since he was faced with a life-threat-ening illness. What he saw was someone who gave lip service to relationships but someone who had never given himself to people other than physically. The depression which followed only began to lift when he entered counselling after leaving hospital. His therapeutic relationship gave him the confidence to change his life and to seek possibilities for positive opportunities for being with other people. At this time he also began to reclaim his spiri-tual life and began attending church again. 'Church became important for me because it was the only time in my week when I could be alone with myself and listen to what God might be saying to me. At one point I thought perhaps I was being called to be a priest, but I soon understood that the call was to be more authentic in my personal life. What that meant for me was developing friendships of equality and love based on mutual caring and support.'

The next five years of John's life were a steady journey towards intimacy with others in a new way. He became a volunteer in a programme to feed homeless young people who were sleeping rough and eventually became the director of the organization. Through his involvement with his church he made new friends who shared common interests in music and drama, and he took up opportunities for travel with the same group of friends. One of the things he valued the most at this time was his role as god-father to two of his friend's children. When he died suddenly of pneumonia in the early 1980s he left behind a group of friends who mourned a man they had come to love. A few weeks before his sudden death, John told his counsellor that he wouldn't trade the previous five years of his life for any other. He talked about the courage it took to reach outside of himself and make positive decisions about change. 'I hardly recognize the person I used to be; I realize now how my self-centredness was a defence against intimacy ... the very thing I said I always wanted. It often felt quite dangerous when I would become close with someone, and sometimes I made mistakes, but I have never regretted fighting the fear which kept me out of relationship with other people.'

The contrasts between Sophie and John are obvious, but the major difference between the two is courage. Sophie is making slow progress through her storm of confusion and pain in mid-life, but she seems to be bound by the pain of her past. The ability gently to let go of the past is an important element in negotiating mid-life change, and one which allows us to begin to grow. The first stage of our lives is definitely over and to enter positively into the second stage there must be a period of mourning for what has gone before. We are no longer young and that fact alone is enough to disempower some people. Sophie is not able to move on or to move beyond her own particular set of problems. She can only focus on her present pain and this prevents her from seeing any possibilities for the future. While she swings from one hope to another she is not able to understand that the answer lies within herself, not in something which will come from the outside to rescue her. John always carried the storm of the first stage of his life with him but was able to see possibilities for change, and like many people in mid-life he saw that the change would involve closer caring relationships with other people. This is often the key which unlocks the door, or the wind of change which calms the storm and allows us to take flight.

The challenge in mid-life can be seen as the choice to be a falcon which can fly through the storm. The fear of what we might find when we attempt the flight can be frightening, but most mid-lifers feel that to remain in the same spot is to die to life. No one knows how much time is left to them, and the positive way to understand this is to live life more fully. The stories in this book present people who have done just that. The authors hope they have been able to convey the excitement and joy which most of the people feel in the second stage of their lives. All of them would say that they have no wish to repeat the past, all of them would say that they have chosen a renewed life, and all of them would say that though they had little idea of what the second stage would be like they are surprised by the joy they have experienced. In fact, to remain with the goals of the first stage of life is a type of death: a denial of the possibilities which remain for us in the second stage of life.

The second stage of life can be the most exciting as we are freed of the agendas and external responsibilities set for us by others.

What can be more exciting than exploring the person God means us to be?

Suggested Reading

Bly, Robert, *Iron John: A Book About Men*, Addison-Wesley Publishing Co., Reading, Mass., 1990

Bradberry, Grace and Justine Hancock, 'Midlife: A Drama Not A Crisis', *The Daily Mail*, London, 24 May 1993

Corneau, Guy, *Absent Fathers, Lost Sons: The Search for Masculine Identity*, Shambhala Publications Ltd., Boston, Mass., 1991

Cavafy, C. P., *The Complete Poems of Cavafy*, Harcourt Brace, London, 1976.

Cupitt, Don, *The Sea of Faith*, SCM Press, London, 1994

Dominian, Jack, *Sexual Integrity*, Darton, Longman & Todd, London, 1987

Greer, Germaine, *The Change*, Hamish Hamilton, London, 1992

Gee, Maggie, *Lost Children*, Flamingo, London, 1994

Hollis, James, *The Middle Passage: From Misery to Meaning in Midlife*, Inner City Books, Toronto, 1993

Houston, J., *In Search of Happiness: A Guide to Personal Contentment*, Lion, London, 1990

Jung, Carl, *The Portable Jung*, Joseph Campbell (ed.), Viking, New York, 1971

Leech, Kenneth, *Soul Friend: A Study of Spirituality*, Sheldon Press, London, 1977

Lerner, Harriet Goldhor, *The Dance of Intimacy*, Harper & Row, London, 1989

McNeill, John J., *The Church and the Homosexual*, Beacon Press, Boston, Mass., 1988

Morely, Robert E., *Intimate Strangers*, Family Welfare Enterprises Ltd., Rugby, 1984

Neustatter, Angela, 'Lost Children and Lost Mothers', *The Independent*, London, 22 April 1994

O'Connor, Peter, *Understanding the Mid-Life Crisis: How Men Go Through Mid-life Upheaval and How They Can Find Healing*, Paulist Press, New York, 1981

Peck, M. Scott, *The Road Less Travelled*, Arrow Books, London, 1978

Pincus, Lily, *Death and the Family*, Faber & Faber, London, 1976

Rilke, Rainer Maria, *Selected Poems of Rainer Maria Rilke*, Robert Bly (trs.), Harper & Row, New York, 1981

Rowe, Dorothy, *Time on Our Side: Growing in Wisdom, Not Growing Old*, HarperCollins Publishers, London, 1994

Shehy, Gail, *Passages*, Bantam Books, London, 1977

Sontag, Susan, 'The Double Standard of Ageing', *The Saturday Review*, October 1972, pp. 29–38

Thatcher, Adrian, *Liberating Sex: A Christian Sexual Theology*, SPCK, London, 1993

Thompson, Jim, *Half Way: Reflections in Mid-Life*, Collins, London, 1986

Turow, Scott, *Pleading Guilty*, Penguin, London, 1994

Viorst, Judith, *Necessary Losses*, Simon & Schuster Ltd., London, 1986

Walrond-Skinner, Sue, *Family Matters*, SPCK, London, 1988